QUICK & EASY

KETOGENIC COOKBOOK

QUICK & EASY KETOGENIC COOKBOOK

13-Digit ISBN: 978-1-64643-050-5

10-Digit ISBN: 1-64643-050-6

This book may be ordered by mail from the publisher. Please include $5.99 for postage and handling. Please support your local bookseller first!

Books published by Cider Mill Press Book Publishers are available at special discounts for bulk purchases in the United States by corporations, institutions, and other organizations. For more information, please contact the publisher.

Cider Mill Press Book Publishers
"Where good books are ready for press"
PO Box 454
12 Spring Street
Kennebunkport, Maine 04046

Typography: Brandon Grotesque, Brothers, Knockout, Archer

Photography: Pages 25, 26, 29, 38, 47, 51, 64, 132, 159, 173, 174, 177, 182, 194, 197, 198, 217, 246, 249, and 250 used under official license from Stockfood. Pages 4-5, 6, 8, 42, 68, 82, 160, 201, and 220 used under official license from Shutterstock. All other photos courtesy of Cider Mill Press.

Front cover image: Chicken Satay Wings, see page 117
Back cover images (top to bottom): Seafood Salad, see page 153;
Barbecue Spareribs, see page 98; Chicken Salad, see page 203
Front endpaper image: Pork Carnitas, see page 102
Back endpaper image: Fried Chicken, see page 137

Printed in China

2 3 4 5 6 7 8 9 0

QUICK & EASY

KETOGENIC COOKBOOK

75+ KETO RECIPES IN 30 MINUTES OR LESS!

CIDER MILL PRESS

BOOK PUBLISHERS

KENNEBUNKPORT, MAINE

CONTENTS

INTRODUCTION

The ketogenic diet goes by many names—low-carb, high fat (LCHF), low-carb, keto—but at its heart the concept remains the same: deprive your body of carbs so it can turn to fat and stored body fat for energy, taking advantage of a process called "ketosis."

Normally, our bodies use glucose as their primary source of energy, derived through the carbohydrates we eat. On the keto diet, we deprive our body of these carbs by limiting consumption of them to under 20 to 30 grams in a day, or roughly 5 percent of our total food intake. When this happens, our body has to find an alternate source of fuel to keep us going, and that is where ketosis kicks in. The liver converts fatty acids into ketone bodies that the brain and other organs can use as fuel.

Keto effectively turns your body into a fat-burning machine, making it a great way to lose weight, while also lowering your overall body fat. But you don't need to have a weight problem to be following the keto diet—a lot of people find that it gives them greater mental clarity, lowers cholesterol and blood pressure, and keeps them away from the processed and sugar-heavy foods that are now known to be at the root of many diseases.

Obviously, keto has myriad benefits.

But, like any diet, it can be tough to stick to considering the unpredictable nature of our lives. And perhaps it is even more so, as one has to keep a close watch over how much protein, fat, and carbs one has consumed each day.

In light of this, we've captured a number of quick and easy dishes that will help you get what you need in no time at all, and ensure that you maintain your progress toward good health, no matter what shape a particular day takes.

It's all here: energy-packed breakfasts, satisfying breads, comforting snacks, and the protein-packed entrees that will help you hit your macros day in and day out. There's even a number of decadent desserts so that you can reward yourself for successfully navigating the sometime-rocky road.

Just like that, all of a sudden, keto doesn't seem so difficult.

BREAKFAST

Keto-friendly breakfast foods are a great way to start the day—so great, in fact, that it seems silly to limit them to a particular time frame. In reality, those foods are all light enough to make for a perfect snack, and substantial enough to give you the lift you're looking for. Whether you're craving something sweet or savory, you're certain to find what you're looking for here, no matter what time of day it is.

BROWN BUTTER SCRAMBLED EGGS

SERVINGS: 1
PREP TIME: 2 MINUTES
COOKING TIME: 5 MINUTES

**NUTRITIONAL INFO:
(PER SERVING)**
CALORIES: 360
NET CARBS: 1 G
CARBS: 1 G
FAT: 34 G
PROTEIN: 13 G
FIBER: 0 G

As eggs are a keto staple, there's always a demand for new and delicious ways to prep them.

1. Whisk the two eggs in a bowl and set aside.

2. Place the butter in a skillet and cook over medium heat until it starts to brown. Reduce heat to the lowest setting and add the eggs, stirring constantly until set, about 3 minutes.

3. Season with salt and pepper, top with chives, and serve with a slice of keto-friendly bread, if desired.

2 eggs

2 tablespoons unsalted butter

Salt and pepper, to taste

Fresh chives, finely chopped

Keto-friendly bread, for serving (optional)

CHEESY FRIED EGGS

SERVINGS: 1
PREP TIME: 2 MINUTES
COOKING TIME: 5 MINUTES

**NUTRITIONAL INFO:
(PER SERVING)**
CALORIES: 241
NET CARBS: 1 G
CARBS: 1 G
FAT: 22 G
PROTEIN: 10 G
FIBER: 0 G

For those who believe the best part of the omelet is the cheese.

1. Place the butter in a skillet and melt it over medium heat.

2. Crack the egg into the pan, top with the cheese, and season with salt and pepper. Reduce the heat to low, cover the pan, and cook until the white is set and the yolk has firmed up, about 2 minutes.

1 tablespoon unsalted butter

1 egg

½ oz. cheddar cheese, grated

Salt and pepper, to taste

EGG & SAUSAGE SANDWICH

SERVINGS: 1
PREP TIME: 5 MINUTES
COOKING TIME: 15 MINUTES

NUTRITIONAL INFO: (PER SERVING)
CALORIES: 732
NET CARBS: 5 G
CARBS: 10 G
FAT: 58 G
PROTEIN: 33 G
FIBER: 5 G

If you still get cravings for a McMuffin now and then, here's a sandwich that fills that void.

1. Place the ground pork, smoked paprika, and oregano in a bowl, season with salt and pepper, and stir to combine. Using your hands, form the mixture into a patty.

2. Place half of the butter in a skillet and melt it over medium heat. Place the patty in the skillet and cook until it is completely cooked through, about 5 minutes per side. Place the cheese on the patty and cook until it is melted. Remove from the pan and tent loosely with aluminum foil to keep warm.

3. Place the remaining butter in the pan. When it has melted, add the egg, prick the yolk, and fry until it has been cooked through. Slice the bread, butter it, and toast it in the pan. Assemble the sandwich and enjoy immediately.

3.5 oz. ground pork

¼ teaspoon smoked paprika

¼ teaspoon dried oregano

Salt and pepper, to taste

½ tablespoon unsalted butter, plus more to taste

1 slice of American cheese

1 egg

1 portion of Coconut Flour Mug Bread (see page 49)

EGGS BENEDICT

SERVINGS: 1
PREP TIME: 5 MINUTES
COOKING TIME: 15 MINUTES

**NUTRITIONAL INFO:
(PER SERVING)**
CALORIES: 301
NET CARBS: 1 G
CARBS: 2.5 G
FAT: 26 G
PROTEIN: 9.5 G
FIBER: 1.5 G

This dish is rich and loaded with fat, and for someone on keto that is a welcome shot in the arm.

1. Spread some of the butter on both sides of the bread. Place a skillet over medium heat and toast the bread in it. Add the ham and cook until it has browned, about 3 minutes.

2. Bring an inch of water to a simmer in a saucepan. Bring water to a boil in another saucepan. Place the lemon juice and egg yolk in a heatproof mixing bowl and whisk to combine. Place the bowl over the simmering water and gradually add the remaining butter, while whisking constantly. When the sauce has thickened, season with salt and pepper and remove it from heat. Leave the bowl over the saucepan to keep the sauce warm.

3. Reduce the heat beneath the other saucepan and crack the egg into the water. Cook until the white is set, about 3 minutes, and remove the egg with a slotted spoon.

4. Place the ham and then the egg on top of the bread. Spoon the hollandaise over the top and garnish with the chives.

   Tip: In the event that your hollandaise sauce separates while the egg is poaching, take a warm bowl, add 1 tablespoon of hot water, and slowly whisk it into the broken hollandaise until it comes together again.

1.4 oz. butter, melted

½ portion of Mug Bread (see page 45)

1 slice of ham

½ teaspoon fresh lemon juice

½ egg yolk

Salt and pepper, to taste

1 egg

Fresh chives, finely chopped, for garnish

PESTO SCRAMBLED EGGS

SERVINGS: 1
PREP TIME: 2 MINUTES
COOKING TIME: 5 MINUTES

**NUTRITIONAL INFO:
(PER SERVING)**
CALORIES: 430
NET CARBS: 1 G
CARBS: 1 G
FAT: 41 G
PROTEIN: 13 G
FIBER: 0 G

Inspired by Dr. Seuss's *Green Eggs and Ham*, these eggs carry a delicious, herbal note thanks to the pesto.

1. Crack the eggs into a bowl, add the cream and pesto, and whisk until the mixture is foamy.

2. Place the butter in a skillet and melt over medium heat. Reduce the heat to the lowest setting, add the eggs, and scramble until they are set, about 5 minutes.

2 eggs

1 tablespoon heavy cream

1 tablespoon Basil Pesto (see page 72)

1 tablespoon unsalted butter

HAM & MUSHROOM OMELET

SERVINGS: 1
PREP TIME: 5 MINUTES
COOKING TIME: 10 MINUTES

NUTRITIONAL INFO:
(PER SERVING)
CALORIES: 516
NET CARBS: 3 G
CARBS: 3 G
FAT: 43 G
PROTEIN: 28 G
FIBER: 0 G

As the look on your loved ones' faces will attest, nothing satisfies quite like this omelet.

1. Place the eggs, salt, pepper, cayenne, and oregano in a bowl and whisk until combined. Add the cream and cheese and whisk to incorporate.

2. Place half of the butter and olive oil in a skillet and warm over medium heat. When the butter starts to foam, add the mushrooms and sauté until they release their liquid, about 3 minutes. Stir in the ham and cook until the mixture starts to brown, about 6 minutes.

3. Reduce the heat to allow, remove the pan from the stove, add the remaining butter and olive oil, and pour in the egg mixture. Swirl to distribute evenly, place the pan back on the stove, cover, and cook until the eggs are set, 1 to 2 minutes. Fold the omelet over and serve.

3 eggs

Salt, to taste

¼ teaspoon black pepper

½ teaspoon cayenne pepper

½ teaspoon dried oregano

2 tablespoons heavy cream

0.7 oz. Swiss cheese, grated

1 tablespoon unsalted butter

1 tablespoon olive oil

0.7 oz. button mushrooms, diced

0.7 oz. ham, cubed

PIZZA OMELET

SERVINGS: 1
PREP TIME: 2 MINUTES
COOKING TIME: 5 MINUTES

NUTRITIONAL INFO:
(PER SERVING)
CALORIES: 504
NET CARBS: 2 G
CARBS: 3 G
FAT: 40 G
PROTEIN: 31 G
FIBER: 1 G

A bit of spicy pepperoni does wonders in transforming what would otherwise be a ho-hum omelet.

1. Place the eggs, salt, pepper, cayenne pepper, and parsley in a bowl and whisk until combined.

2. Place the oil in a cast-iron skillet and warm it over medium heat. Add the egg mixture and top it with the salami, mushrooms, and cheese. Place the skillet in the oven, turn on the broiler, and cook until the eggs are set and the cheese has melted, 5 to 7 minutes.

3 eggs

Salt and pepper, to taste

Pinch of cayenne pepper

Pinch of finely chopped fresh parsley

2 teaspoons olive oil

0.8 oz. pepperoni or salami, sliced

½ oz. white mushrooms, sliced

1 oz. mozzarella or cheddar cheese, grated

FRITTATA BITES

SERVINGS: 6
PREP TIME: 5 MINUTES
COOKING TIME: 25 MINUTES

NUTRITIONAL INFO:
(PER SERVING)
CALORIES: 243
NET CARBS: 2.5 G
CARBS: 3.2 G
FAT: 17.6 G
PROTEIN: 17.7 G
FIBER: 0.7 G

You can also make this as one large frittata, but these bites are more fun, and make it far easier to control your portion size.

1. Preheat the oven to 350°F. Line six wells of a muffin tin with paper wrappers. Place the oil in a skillet and warm over medium heat. When the oil starts to shimmer, add the mushrooms and cook until they start to brown, about 5 minutes. Remove the pan from heat.

2. Place the eggs, almond milk, Parmesan, salt, and black pepper in a mixing bowl and stir to combine. Stir in the red pepper and then divide the mixture between the paper wrappers.

3. Place in the oven and bake for about 20 minutes, until the frittatas are set, golden brown, and puffy. Remove from the oven and let them cool briefly before sprinkling the herbs over each frittata.

2 tablespoons olive oil

8 oz. cremini mushrooms, quartered

12 large eggs

⅔ cup unsweetened almond milk

0.8 oz. Parmesan cheese, grated

½ teaspoon kosher salt

¼ teaspoon black pepper

1 red bell pepper, stemmed, seeded, and diced

2 tablespoons finely chopped fresh thyme

2 tablespoons finely chopped fresh chives

GOLDEN MILK

SERVINGS: 2
PREP TIME: 5 MINUTES
COOKING TIME: 10 MINUTES

**NUTRITIONAL INFO:
(PER SERVING)**
CALORIES: 50
NET CARBS: 2 G
CARBS: 3.9 G
FAT: 4.6 G
PROTEIN: 1.5 G
FIBER: 1.9 G

The wellness community has been trumpeting the healing properties of turmeric for some time. It helps that it's unique flavor also happens to be delicious.

1. Place ¼ cup of the almond milk, the turmeric root, ground turmeric, ground ginger, cinnamon, and cardamom pods in a saucepan and warm over medium heat, whisking occasionally, until a smooth paste forms.

2. Whisk in 1¾ cups of the almond milk while pouring in a slow, steady stream. Bring to a simmer and cook until the mixture is warmed through but not boiling, 3 to 4 minutes. Strain the milk into the serving glasses and stir the sweetener into each.

3. Pour the remaining almond milk into a small saucepan and bring it to a simmer over medium heat. Froth it with a milk frother and spoon it on top of each beverage. Dust with additional ground turmeric and serve.

2⅓ cups unsweetened almond milk

2 teaspoons fresh turmeric root, peeled and grated

1 teaspoon ground turmeric, plus more for garnish

⅛ teaspoon ground ginger

⅛ teaspoon cinnamon

3 cardamom pods, lightly crushed

1 teaspoon stevia or preferred keto-friendly sweetener

MUESLI WITH ALMONDS & KIWI

SERVINGS: 4
PREP TIME: 5 MINUTES
COOKING TIME: N/A

NUTRITIONAL INFO:
(PER SERVING)
CALORIES: 442
NET CARBS: 15.1 G
CARBS: 19.5 G
FAT: 36.2 G
PROTEIN: 9.8 G
FIBER: 4.4 G

Fruit is typically a stay-away on keto, but when paired with nuts and sour cream, it becomes a great way to hit your fat macros.

1. Place the sour cream and cream in a small bowl and stir to combine. Gradually add the sweetener, while stirring to incorporate.

2. Divide the almonds, dates, and golden raisins between the serving dishes. Top each portion with some of the sour cream mixture and kiwi puree and garnish with a sprig of mint.

1½ cups sour cream

3 tablespoons heavy cream

1 tablespoon stevia or preferred keto-friendly sweetener

1.7 oz. blanched almonds

2 large dates, pitted

2 tablespoons golden raisins

2 kiwi, peeled, diced, and pureed

4 sprigs of fresh mint

ALMOND FLOUR PANCAKES

SERVINGS: 4
(1 SERVING = 1 PANCAKE)
PREP TIME: 5 MINUTES
COOKING TIME: 15 MINUTES

**NUTRITIONAL INFO:
(PER SERVING)**
CALORIES: 266
NET CARBS: 3 G
CARBS: 6 G
FAT: 23 G
PROTEIN: 10 G
FIBER: 3 G

These pancakes are nutty, fluffy, and the perfect vehicle for butter and sugar-free maple syrup.

1. Microwave the cream cheese on medium for 30 seconds. Remove, add the heavy cream to the bowl, and whisk to combine. Let the mixture cool.

2. Add the eggs and vanilla and stir until thoroughly combined. Add the remaining ingredients, except for those designated for serving or garnish, and stir until combined.

3. Warm a nonstick skillet over medium heat and grease it with nonstick cooking spray. Ladle ¼-cup portions of the batter into the skillet and cook until set and browned, about 2 minutes. For fluffier pancakes, cover the skillet as they cook. Turn the pancakes over and cook until cooked through, another 2 minutes. Serve with butter and sugar-free maple syrup and garnish with the slices of strawberry.

1.75 oz. cream cheese

1.75 oz. heavy cream

2 eggs

1 teaspoon pure vanilla extract

3.5 oz. almond flour

½ teaspoon baking powder

Pinch of kosher salt

1 teaspoon pumpkin spice mix (optional)

2 to 3 drops of liquid stevia, powdered erythritol, or other keto-friendly sweetener

Butter, for serving

Sugar-free maple syrup, for serving

1 strawberry, sliced, for garnish

COCONUT FLOUR PANCAKES

SERVINGS: 5
(1 SERVING = 1 PANCAKE)

PREP TIME: 5 MINUTES

COOKING TIME: 20 MINUTES

**NUTRITIONAL INFO:
(PER SERVING)**

CALORIES: 221

NET CARBS: 3 G

CARBS: 7 G

FAT: 18 G

PROTEIN: 6 G

FIBER: 4 G

These light and fluffy pancakes are a great snack on the go.

1. Sift the coconut flour, baking powder, cinnamon, and salt into a mixing bowl, stir to combine, and set the mixture aside.

2. Place the butter and cream cheese in a microwave-safe bowl and microwave on medium for 30 seconds. Remove, add the cream, and whisk to combine. Let the mixture cool slightly. Once the mixture has cooled slightly, stir in the eggs, vanilla extract, and sweetener.

3. Add the dry mixture to the wet mixture and whisk until a smooth batter forms. Place a nonstick skillet over medium heat and grease it with nonstick cooking spray. Ladle ¼-cup portions of the batter into the skillet, cover it, and cook until set and browned, about 2 minutes. Flip the pancakes over and cook until cooked through, another 2 minutes. Serve with sugar-free maple syrup and butter or fresh berries and whipped cream.

0.8 oz. coconut flour

½ teaspoon baking powder

½ teaspoon cinnamon

Pinch of kosher salt

1.75 oz. butter, more for serving optional

1.75 oz. cream cheese

1.75 oz. heavy cream

3 eggs

½ teaspoon pure vanilla extract

2 to 3 drops liquid stevia or preferred keto-friendly sweetener

Sugar-free maple syrup, for serving (optional)

Fresh berries, for serving (optional)

Sugar-free whipped cream, for serving (optional)

ALMOND FLOUR WAFFLES

SERVINGS: 1
PREP TIME: 5 MINUTES
COOKING TIME: 5 MINUTES

NUTRITIONAL INFO:
(PER SERVING)
CALORIES: 586
NET CARBS: 8 G
CARBS: 13 G
FAT: 52 G
PROTEIN: 13 G
FIBER: 5 G

These waffles lean toward the savory side, and are actually lovely with some Basil Pesto (see page 72) spread on them.

1. Preheat a waffle iron and grease it with nonstick cooking spray. Place all of the ingredients, except for the syrup and butter, in a bowl and whisk until a smooth batter forms.

2. Working in batches, pour the batter into a waffle iron and cook until crispy and golden brown, 2 to 3 minutes. Serve with syrup and butter or use them to make a waffle-wich.

1.75 oz. almond flour

0.7 oz. cheddar cheese, grated

¼ cup heavy cream

½ teaspoon baking powder

¼ teaspoon kosher salt

2 to 3 drops of stevia

1 egg

Sugar-free maple syrup, for serving

Butter, for serving

PEANUT BUTTER WAFFLES

SERVINGS: 2
(1 SERVING = 1 WAFFLE)
PREP TIME: 5 MINUTES
COOKING TIME: 10 MINUTES

NUTRITIONAL INFO:
(PER SERVING)
CALORIES: 481
NET CARBS: 7 G
CARBS: 11 G
FAT: 43 G
PROTEIN: 18 G
FIBER: 4 G

These waffles are as good as—if not better than—non-ketofied waffles, and the peanut butter adds a delicious nuttiness.

1. Preheat a waffle iron and grease it with nonstick cooking spray. Place the peanut butter, butter, and cream cheese in a microwave-safe bowl and microwave on medium for 30 seconds. Remove, add the cream, baking powder, and sweetener and stir until thoroughly combined.

2. Add the eggs and whisk until the mixture is a smooth, thick batter. Working in batches, ladle the batter into the waffle iron and cook until crispy and golden brown, 2 to 3 minutes. Serve with the sugar-free maple syrup and additional butter.

2.8 oz. natural, no sugar added peanut butter

2 tablespoons unsalted butter, plus more for serving

1.4 oz. cream cheese

1.4 oz. heavy cream

½ teaspoon baking powder

Stevia or preferred keto-friendly sweetener, to taste

2 eggs

Sugar-free maple syrup, for serving

ALMOND FLOUR & FLAXSEED MUFFINS

SERVINGS: 6
PREP TIME: 5 MINUTES
COOKING TIME: 25 MINUTES

**NUTRITIONAL INFO:
(PER SERVING)**
CALORIES: 206
NET CARBS: 3.5 G
CARBS: 6.8 G
FAT: 18.2 G
PROTEIN: 7.1 G
FIBER: 3.3 G

The flaxseeds give these muffins a wholesome shot of beneficial Omega-3 fatty acids.

1. Preheat the oven to 350°F. Line a muffin or cupcake tin with paper wrappers.

2. Sift the almond flour, baking powder, salt, and spices into a mixing bowl. Stir in the flaxseed meal and sweetener. Place the almond milk, eggs, and coconut oil in a separate bowl and whisk to combine. Add the mixture to the dry ingredients and stir until the batter just comes together; it shouldn't be totally smooth.

3. Divide the batter between the wrappers and gently shake the pan to evenly distribute the batter. Place the muffins in the oven and bake for about 20 minutes, until they have risen, are dry to the touch, and a toothpick inserted into the center of each one comes out clean. Remove from the oven and let them cool in the pan before serving.

5 oz. almond flour

½ tablespoon baking powder

¼ teaspoon kosher salt

¼ teaspoon cinnamon

¼ teaspoon grated fresh nutmeg

2 tablespoons golden flaxseed meal

2 tablespoons stevia or preferred keto-friendly sweetener

¼ cup unsweetened almond milk

2 small eggs

2 tablespoons coconut oil, melted

LEMON & POPPY SEED MUFFINS

SERVINGS: 8
(1 SERVING = 1 MUFFIN)
PREP TIME: 5 MINUTES
COOKING TIME: 25 MINUTES

NUTRITIONAL INFO:
(PER SERVING)
CALORIES: 226
NET CARBS: 3 G
CARBS: 5 G
FAT: 21 G
PROTEIN: 7 G
FIBER: 2 G

These muffins can be made ahead and frozen, so you can defrost one when you need it.

---

1. Preheat the oven to 345°F and line a muffin tin with paper wrappers. Place the almond flour, poppy seeds, baking powder, salt, and lemon zest in a mixing bowl and stir to combine.

2. Place the butter and sweetener in a mixing bowl and beat it with a handheld mixer until pale and fluffy. If using a granulated sweetener, pulse 3 or 4 times in the blender before adding it to the butter so that it has an easier time dissolving.

3. Add the sour cream to the butter mixture and whisk to incorporate. Whisk in the vanilla, eggs, and lemon juice and then add the dry mixture. Stir until a smooth batter forms. Divide the batter between the wrappers, filling each compartment two-thirds of the way.

4. Place in the oven and bake for about 25 minutes, until the muffins are golden brown and a toothpick inserted into the center of each one comes out clean. Remove from the oven and let cool slightly before serving.

4.9 oz. almond flour

1½ tablespoons poppy seeds

½ teaspoon baking powder

Salt, to taste

Juice and zest of 1 lemon

6 tablespoons unsalted butter

3.5 oz. Sukrin Gold or preferred keto-friendly sweetener

3 oz. sour cream

½ teaspoon pure vanilla extract

2 eggs

BREADS & CRACKERS

The process of transforming one's health via the ketogenic diet means that you have to leave those beloved, gluten and carb–loaded loaves of bread behind. Keto bread does not taste like that—but that doesn't mean that it tastes bad. It's just different, as its reliance on eggs and nut flours produces breads that are more like cake than bread, and, as you'll see, these denser and more nutritious loaves are plenty delicious. There's also a couple of cracker recipes for those times when you just want to kick back, and snack.

MUG BREAD

SERVINGS: 1
PREP TIME: 2 MINUTES
COOKING TIME: 2 MINUTES

NUTRITIONAL INFO: (PER SERVING)
CALORIES: 324
NET CARBS: 2 G
CARBS: 5 G
FAT: 28 G
PROTEIN: 13 G
FIBER: 3 G

Baking bread is a time-consuming process for people with fast-paced lives. Not anymore, as this bread takes less than 5 minutes.

1. Place all of the ingredients in a large mug and stir to combine.

2. Place the mug in the microwave and microwave on medium for 1½ minutes. Remove, turn the mug over, and tap it until the bread slides out.

1 oz. almond flour

1 tablespoon olive oil

½ teaspoon baking powder

1 egg

KETO WRAPS

SERVINGS: 8
PREP TIME: 5 MINUTES
COOKING TIME: 20 MINUTES

**NUTRITIONAL INFO:
(PER SERVING)**

CALORIES: 41

NET CARBS: 0.7 G

CARBS: 1.5 G

FAT: 2 G

PROTEIN: 3.9 G

FIBER: 0.8 G

Don't overlook these light and lovely wraps. They are delicious, and a lifesaver when you need something in a pinch.

1. Place all of the ingredients, except for the olive oil, in a mixing bowl and stir until the mixture is a smooth batter.

2. Coat the bottom of a cast-iron skillet with some of the olive oil and warm over medium heat. When the oil starts to shimmer, ladle a small amount of the batter into the pan and tilt the pan to coat the surface entirely. Cook until the bottom of the wrap is set and golden brown, 2 to 3 minutes. Flip the wrap over and cook for another minute. Place the cooked wrap on a plate, cover with aluminum foil, and repeat the process until all of the batter has been used.

8 large egg whites

1 oz. coconut flour

⅔ cup water

¼ teaspoon baking powder

¼ teaspoon kosher salt

½ oz. fresh mint leaves, finely chopped

1 tablespoon olive oil

COCONUT FLOUR MUG BREAD

SERVINGS: 1
PREP TIME: 2 MINUTES
COOKING TIME: 2 MINUTES

NUTRITIONAL INFO:
(PER SERVING)
CALORIES: 286
NET CARBS: 4 G
CARBS: 9 G
FAT: 24 G
PROTEIN: 8 G
FIBER: 5 G

Almond flour can get expensive as an everyday ingredient. Luckily, this bread speeds to the rescue.

---

1. Place all of the ingredients in a large mug and stir until thoroughly combined.

2. Place the mug in the microwave and microwave for 1½ minutes. Remove the mug, turn it over, and tap it until the bread slides out.

1 oz. coconut flour

1 tablespoon heavy cream

1 tablespoon olive oil

1 egg

¼ teaspoon baking powder

Salt, to taste

CLOUD BREAD

SERVINGS: 8
PREP TIME: 10 MINUTES
COOKING TIME: 35 MINUTES

NUTRITIONAL INFO:
(PER SERVING)
CALORIES: 61
NET CARBS: 0.6 G
CARBS: 0.6 G
FAT: 4.9 G
PROTEIN: 3.7 G
FIBER: 0 G

Should you have a hankering for a sandwich, this bread is your best bet.

1. Preheat the oven to 300°F. Place the egg yolks and cream cheese in a mixing bowl and beat until smooth.

2. Place the egg whites, salt, and cream of tartar in a separate bowl and mix until soft, fluffy peaks form. Fold the mixture into the egg yolk mixture.

3. Grease two large baking sheets with nonstick cooking spray. Spoon eight mounds of the mixture onto the sheets, leaving plenty of space between.

4. Place in the oven and bake for about 35 minutes, until the slices are golden brown. Remove from the oven and let cool on the baking sheets before using.

4 large eggs, yolks and whites separated

2 oz. cream cheese, at room temperature

Pinch of kosher salt

¼ teaspoon cream of tartar

BREAD CRUMBS

SERVINGS: 1
PREP TIME: 5 MINUTES
COOKING TIME: 1 TO 2 HOURS

**NUTRITIONAL INFO:
(PER SERVING)**
CALORIES: 324
NET CARBS: 2 G
CARBS: 5 G
FAT: 28 G
PROTEIN: 13 G
FIBER: 3 G

This recipe is perfect for fried chicken, fish, or anything else that needs a satisfying crunch.

1. Preheat the oven to 245°F. Slice the bread, place it on a baking sheet, and bake for 1 to 2 hours, until the bread is dry and crumbly.

2. Remove from the oven and let cool completely. Place the bread in a food processor and blitz until it is crumbs. Store in an airtight container until ready to use.

1 portion of Mug Bread (see page 45)

CAULIFLOWER BREAD

SERVINGS: 4
PREP TIME: 15 MINUTES
COOKING TIME: 35 MINUTES

NUTRITIONAL INFO:
(PER SERVING)
CALORIES: 80
NET CARBS: 2 G
CARBS: 3.5 G
FAT: 5.5 G
PROTEIN: 5 G
FIBER: 1.5 G

Not only is this a less caloric bread than most keto options, it also makes for excellent hamburger buns.

1. Preheat the oven to 375°F and line a baking sheet with parchment paper. Place the cauliflower florets in a food processor and blitz until they are rice-like in consistency.

2. Place the cauliflower in a microwave-safe bowl and microwave on medium for 5 to 7 minutes, until tender. Place the cauliflower in a kitchen towel and wring the towel to remove as much liquid as possible.

3. Place the cauliflower in a bowl with the salt, pepper, Parmesan cheese, cream cheese, and egg. Divide the mixture into four portions and shape them into rounds on the baking sheet.

4. Place in the oven and bake for 20 to 25 minutes, until cooked through and golden brown. Remove from the oven and let cool completely. Reserve any leftover cauliflower for another preparation.

6.3 oz. cauliflower florets

Salt and pepper, to taste

0.8 oz. Parmesan cheese, grated

1 oz. cream cheese, at room temperature

1 egg

COCONUT FLOUR BREAD

SERVINGS: 12
(1 SERVING = 1 SLICE)
PREP TIME: 10 MINUTES
COOKING TIME: 50 MINUTES

NUTRITIONAL INFO:
(PER SERVING)
CALORIES: 174
NET CARBS: 2 G
CARBS: 4 G
FAT: 15 G
PROTEIN: 7 G
FIBER: 2 G

This loaf comes out nice and fluffy thanks to the xanthan gum and psyllium husk, and it is even better when toasted.

1. Preheat the oven to 325°F. Line a 9 x 5–inch loaf pan with parchment paper and grease it with nonstick cooking spray.

2. Place the coconut flour, xanthan gum, psyllium husk, baking powder, and salt in a bowl and stir to combine. In another bowl, whisk together the eggs and olive oil. Working in three increments, add the dry mixture and incorporate each portion thoroughly before adding the next. Add the water and whisk until the mixture is a smooth batter.

3. Pour the batter into the pan, place it in the oven, and bake for 40 to 50 minutes, until a toothpick inserted into the center of the loaf comes out clean. Remove and let the bread cool before removing it from the pan.

2.6 oz. coconut flour

1 teaspoon xanthan gum

½ oz. psyllium husk

1 teaspoon baking powder

½ teaspoon kosher salt

6 eggs

6 tablespoons olive oil

½ cup warm water (110°F)

PEANUT BUTTER BREAD

SERVINGS: 20
(1 SERVING = 1 SLICE)
PREP TIME: 10 MINUTES
COOKING TIME: 40 MINUTES

NUTRITIONAL INFO:
(PER SERVING)
CALORIES: 86
NET CARBS: 2 G
CARBS: 3 G
FAT: 7 G
PROTEIN: 4 G
FIBER: 1 G

Peanut butter is keto's magic bullet. This loaf is a nutty delight that makes the most decadent French toast.

1. Preheat the oven to 325°F and grease a 9 x 5–inch loaf pan with nonstick cooking spray. Place all of the ingredients in a mixing bowl and work the mixture until a smooth dough forms.

2. Place the dough in the greased pan, place it in the oven, and bake for 25 minutes, until a toothpick inserted into the center comes out clean. Remove and let cool briefly before slicing and serving.

Tip: This dough is quite thick and sticky and can be hard to work with, but it comes together with a bit of elbow grease and patience.

8.8 oz. natural, no sugar added peanut butter

3 eggs

1 teaspoon white vinegar

½ teaspoon baking soda

Stevia or preferred keto-friendly sweetener, to taste

Pinch of kosher salt

FATHEAD CRUST PIZZA

SERVINGS: 1
PREP TIME: 5 MINUTES
COOKING TIME: 25 MINUTES

NUTRITIONAL INFO:
(PER SERVING)
CALORIES: 705
NET CARBS: 10 G
CARBS: 15 G
FAT: 57 G
PROTEIN: 38 G
FIBER: 5 G

Cauliflower pizza is great but it can be a bit finicky to make. This crust definitely rivals (and probably beats out) the cauliflower crust thanks to its crispy finish and filling ingredients. It's also much easier to make, but the calorie and carb count may just put the cauliflower crust back in the lead. Try both and see which you like best.

1. Preheat the oven to 390°F. Place the mozzarella and cream cheese in a microwave-safe bowl and microwave for 1 minute. Stir to combine, season with salt and garlic powder, and stir in the almond flour.

2. Microwave for another 30 seconds, remove, and let cool slightly. Add the egg and stir until thoroughly combined. Place the dough on a parchment-lined baking sheet and gently pat it into a circle.

3. Place in the oven and bake for 15 minutes. Remove from the oven, flip the crust over, and spread the sauce on top. Distribute the ham, pepperoni, and mushrooms over the sauce, turn on the broiler, and broil until the toppings are warmed through and the cheese (if using as a topping) is melted. Remove and let cool briefly before slicing and serving.

3.5 oz. mozzarella cheese, grated

0.8 oz. cream cheese

1 teaspoon garlic powder

Salt, to taste

1.75 oz. almond flour

1 egg

Marinara Sauce (see page 75), to taste

0.8 oz. ham

0.8 oz. pepperoni

0.8 oz. mushrooms, sliced

ALMOND FLOUR ROLLS

SERVINGS: 6
(1 SERVING = 1 ROLL)
PREP TIME: 10 MINUTES
COOKING TIME: 15 MINUTES

**NUTRITIONAL INFO:
(PER SERVING)**
CALORIES: 141
NET CARBS: 1 G
CARBS: 2 G
FAT: 13 G
PROTEIN: 4 G
FIBER: 1 G

The fluffy bread used to mop up pav bhaji, a beloved street food in Mumbai, served as the inspiration for these rolls.

1. Preheat the oven to 355°F and grease a muffin tin with nonstick cooking spray. Microwave the cream cheese for 30 seconds. Add the olive oil to the bowl and stir until combined.

2. Add the almond flour, baking powder, and salt and stir until combined. Let the mixture cool slightly and then whisk in the egg yolks.

3. Place the egg whites and cream of tartar in a separate bowl and whisk until stiff peaks form. Working in three increments, fold the egg white mixture into the cream cheese mixture.

4. Distribute the mixture in the muffin tin, place it in the oven, and bake for 12 to 15 minutes, until the rolls are puffy and golden brown. Remove and let cool briefly before serving.

1.75 oz. cream cheese

2 tablespoons olive oil

1.75 oz. almond flour

½ teaspoon baking powder

Salt, to taste

2 eggs, yolks and whites separated

¼ teaspoon cream of tartar

MULTI-SEED CRACKERS

SERVINGS: 12
PREP TIME: 5 MINUTES
COOKING TIME: 3 HOURS AND 30 MINUTES

NUTRITIONAL INFO: (PER SERVING)
CALORIES: 173
NET CARBS: 4 G
CARBS: 8.2 G
FAT: 14.4 G
PROTEIN: 5.3 G
FIBER: 4.2 G

By virtue of the numerous nutrient-packed seeds, these crackers are not only delicious, they are a great way to get additional vitamins.

1. Preheat the oven to 225°F. Line a large baking sheet with parchment paper. Place all of the seeds, the almonds, and the water in a large bowl, stir, and let the mixture stand for 20 minutes. Whisk in the salt and set the mixture aside.

2. Grease the parchment paper with a little bit of the coconut oil. Spread the mixture on the baking sheet in a thin, even layer. Brush the top with the remaining coconut oil, place in the oven, and bake for 1 hour and 45 minutes.

3. Remove from the oven, carefully flip the cracker over, and peel away the parchment paper. Return to the oven and bake for another 1 hour and 45 minutes.

4. Remove from the oven and let cool for 10 minutes before cutting out round crackers from the sheet. Let the crackers cool completely on wire racks before serving.

3.75 oz. sesame seeds

1.3 oz. golden linseeds

2.35 oz. shelled sunflower seeds

3 tablespoons pumpkin seeds

2 tablespoons flaxseeds

2 tablespoons chopped almonds

1⅔ cups water

1½ teaspoons kosher salt

3 tablespoons coconut oil, melted

FATHEAD CRACKERS

SERVINGS: 8
(1 SERVING = 1 CRACKER)
PREP TIME: 5 MINUTES
COOKING TIME: 15 MINUTES

NUTRITIONAL INFO:
(PER SERVING)
CALORIES: 88
NET CARBS: 1 G
CARBS: 2 G
FAT: 8 G
PROTEIN: 4 G
FIBER: 1 G

These crackers are cheesy and crunchy, perfect for keto-safe snacking.

1. Preheat the oven to 390°F and line a baking sheet with parchment paper. Place the mozzarella and cream cheese in a bowl and microwave for about 1 minute, until the mozzarella is fully melted.

2. Remove and stir with a rubber spatula. Stir in the salt, pepper, and parsley, add the almond flour, and knead the mixture until a smooth dough forms.

3. Place the dough between two sheets of parchment paper and roll it thin.

4. Place the dough on the baking sheet, place it in the oven, and bake for 10 minutes, until golden brown. Remove, transfer the crackers to a wire rack, and cut them into desired shapes when they have cooled slightly.

3.5 oz. mozzarella cheese, grated

1.4 oz. cream cheese

Salt and pepper, to taste

1 tablespoon finely chopped fresh parsley

1.75 oz. almond flour

SAUCES & DIPS

The shortest chapter in the book, but perhaps also the most important. Delicious, keto-friendly sauces and dips are a snap to make, and will work their way into many of the dishes in this book. Once you get a handle on those, turn to this chapter, and see what recipes you can use to put a twist on some of your favorites, or to provide a lift to those preparations you've always suspected could be so much more.

BARBECUE SAUCE

SERVINGS: 20
(1 SERVING = 1 TABLESPOON)
PREP TIME: 10 MINUTES
COOKING TIME: 20 MINUTES

NUTRITIONAL INFO:
(PER SERVING)
CALORIES: 25
NET CARBS: 1 G
CARBS: 1 G
FAT: 2 G
PROTEIN: 0 G
FIBER: 0 G

Slather this on Bacon Bomb Balls (see page 94), toss it on pulled pork, or used it to baste a whole roast chicken. The possibilities are endless, as is the flavor.

1. Place the butter in a saucepan and melt it over low heat. Add the onion and garlic and cook until the onion starts to soften, about 6 minutes. Add the salt, black pepper, paprika, cayenne, and cumin and cook for 2 minutes.

2. Stir in the tomatoes, balsamic vinegar, sweetener, and Worcestershire sauce, cover the pot, and cook for 7 to 8 minutes.

3. Transfer the mixture to a food processor or blender and puree the mixture until smooth. Return the mixture to the saucepan, add the mustard, apple cider vinegar, and hot sauce and cook until the mixture reaches the desired consistency. Let cool completely before using or storing. The sauce will keep in the refrigerator for up to 2 weeks.

1.75 oz. unsalted butter

2.8 oz. onion

5 garlic cloves

1 teaspoon kosher salt

1 teaspoon black pepper

1 teaspoon paprika

1 teaspoon cayenne pepper

1 teaspoon cumin

5.3 oz. tomatoes, diced

1 teaspoon balsamic vinegar

1 teaspoon stevia or preferred keto-friendly sweetener

1 teaspoon Worcestershire sauce

1 tablespoon yellow mustard

2.1 oz. apple cider vinegar

1 tablespoon sriracha or preferred hot sauce

BASIL PESTO

SERVINGS: 12
(1 SERVING = ABOUT 0.5 OZ.)
PREP TIME: 2 MINUTES
COOKING TIME: 2 MINUTES

**NUTRITIONAL INFO:
(PER SERVING)**
CALORIES: 142
NET CARBS: 0 G
CARBS: 0 G
FAT: 16 G
PROTEIN: 2 G
FIBER: 0 G

Don't skimp on the quality of the olive oil in this one—that's the one thing you should never compromise on when making pesto.

1. Place the Parmesan, pine nuts, garlic, parsley, and basil in a food processor and puree until smooth.

2. Place the mixture in a bowl, and gradually add the olive oil while whisking to incorporate it. Stir in the lemon juice, season with salt, and serve.

1 oz. Parmesan cheese, grated

0.7 oz. pine nuts

2 garlic cloves, minced

1 oz. fresh parsley

1.75 oz. fresh basil leaves

¾ cup olive oil

½ tablespoon fresh lemon juice

Salt, to taste

MARINARA SAUCE

SERVINGS: 8
(1 SERVING = 2 OZ.)
PREP TIME: 10 MINUTES
COOKING TIME: 20 MINUTES

NUTRITIONAL INFO:
(PER SERVING)
CALORIES: 71
NET CARBS: 1 G
CARBS: 2 G
FAT: 7 G
PROTEIN: 1 G
FIBER: 1 G

Marinara is the foundation of Italian cuisine and a good marinara is integral to so many keto recipes, from pizza and zoodles (aka zucchini noodles) to chicken Parmesan and eggplant lasagna. This recipe cuts out the extra sugars and additives and adds in some fat, resulting in a keto-friendly, versatile sauce that you'll be tempted to eat right out of the jar.

1. Place the olive oil in a saucepan and warm over medium heat. When the oil starts to shimmer, add the onion, season with salt, and sauté until the onion turns translucent, about 3 minutes.

2. Add the garlic, season with red pepper flakes, and cook until the onion starts to brown, about 6 minutes. Stir in the tomatoes, season with salt and pepper, cover the pan, and cook until the oil rises to the top, 10 to 12 minutes. Stir in the basil and oregano and cook for another 2 minutes.

3. Stir in the butter and use immediately.

2 tablespoons olive oil

1.75 oz. diced red onion

Salt and pepper , to taste

2 garlic cloves, minced

Red pepper flakes, to taste

14 oz. tomatoes, chopped

1 handful of fresh basil, chopped

5 tablespoons finely chopped fresh oregano

1 tablespoon unsalted butter

BOLOGNESE SAUCE

SERVINGS: 6
PREP TIME: 5 MINUTES
COOKING TIME: 25 MINUTES

NUTRITIONAL INFO:
(PER SERVING)
CALORIES: 28
NET CARBS: 3 G
CARBS: 5 G
FAT: 22 G
PROTEIN: 18 G
FIBER: 2 G

The wine that is traditionally a part of this sauce is left out to keep the carb counts low, but otherwise this is the sauce you know and love.

1. Place the olive oil and butter in saucepan and warm over medium heat. When the butter starts to foam, add the red onion and cook until it is translucent, about 3 minutes. Add the ground beef and pork and cook, using a wooden spoon to break it up, until it starts to brown, about 6 minutes. Season with salt, pepper, chili flakes, and oregano, add the thyme and garlic, and cook for 2 to 3 minutes.

2. Add the mushrooms, tomatoes, water, and bouillon cube, cover the pan, and cook for 15 minutes, stirring occasionally. Add the water as needed if the pan starts to look dry.

3. Stir in the spinach, cover the pan, and cook until the spinach has wilted, 1 to 2 minutes. Add the cream and parsley, cook until the sauce is warmed through, and use immediately.

1 tablespoon olive oil

1 tablespoon unsalted butter

1.75 oz. red onion, grated

8.8 oz. ground beef

8.8 oz. ground pork

Salt and pepper, to taste

Red pepper flakes, to taste

Dried oregano, to taste

Leaves from 2 sprigs of fresh thyme

4 garlic cloves, minced

3.5 oz. button mushrooms, chopped

3.5 oz. tomatoes, diced

¼ cup water

1 cube of beef or chicken bouillon

3.5 oz. baby spinach

3.5 oz. heavy cream

¼ cup finely chopped fresh parsley

BABA GHANOUSH

SERVINGS: 8
(1 SERVING = 2.4 OZ.)
PREP TIME: 15 MINUTES
COOKING TIME: 20 MINUTES

NUTRITIONAL INFO:
(PER SERVING)
CALORIES: 95
NET CARBS: 4 G
CARBS: 6 G
FAT: 7 G
PROTEIN: 2 G
FIBER: 2 G

Eggplant's meaty texture is at its best roasted, as this dip proves.

1. Preheat the oven to 400°F. Pierce the skin of the eggplant with a knife or fork and place it on a baking sheet. Place it in the oven and roast for about 25 minutes, until the skin is blistered and the flesh is tender. Remove from the oven and let cool.

2. Peel the eggplant and chop the flesh. Place it in a bowl with the remaining ingredients, except for the parsley, and stir to combine. Garnish with the parsley and serve.

   Tip: For a creamier texture, use a food processor or blender to puree the eggplant.

17.6 oz. eggplant

2 garlic cloves, diced

1.75 oz. tahini

½ teaspoon fresh lemon juice

1 teaspoon kosher salt

½ teaspoon cumin

½ teaspoon paprika

¼ teaspoon cayenne pepper

2 tablespoons olive oil

1 tablespoon finely chopped fresh parsley, for garnish

CAULIFLOWER HUMMUS

SERVINGS: 12
PREP TIME: 5 MINUTES
COOKING TIME: 10 MINUTES

NUTRITIONAL INFO:
(PER SERVING)
CALORIES: 150
NET CARBS: 3 G
CARBS: 5 G
FAT: 14 G
PROTEIN: 2 G
FIBER: 2 G

Apart from being the new potato and the new rice, cauliflower is also the new chickpea—softened, boiled cauliflower, when pureed, makes a rich and creamy hummus.

1. Bring salted water to a boil in a large saucepan, add the cauliflower, and cook until it is tender, about 10 minutes.

2. Place the cauliflower in a food processor, add the remaining ingredients, except for the parsley, and blitz until the mixture is very smooth. Sprinkle the parsley on top and serve.

Salt and pepper, to taste

17.6 oz. cauliflower, trimmed

2.1 oz. tahini

3 garlic cloves, minced

½ cup olive oil

3.5 oz. pitted Kalamata olives

1 teaspoon paprika

1 teaspoon cumin

Juice of 1 lemon

1 tablespoon finely chopped fresh parsley

PROTEIN-PACKED

Hitting your macros is as important a part of keto as limiting calories and carbs. In order to make sure you are burning fat at an optimal rate, you need to make sure your body is getting enough protein, a metric that isn't always easy to hit considering the breakneck pace the world now moves at, and the millions of unexpected directions that current can pull you in. You can relax, though—now that these dishes are on your side, you're sure to hit your marks.

BOUQUET GARNI

This handy little spice sack will save you a ton of prep time. To make one, simply cut out a square of cheesecloth, place fresh parsley, thyme, rosemary, and bay leaves in it, and roll up the cheesecloth. Tie off the ends and it's ready to use.

BEEF BOURGUIGNON

SERVINGS: 5
PREP TIME: 10 MINUTES
COOKING TIME: 2 HOURS

NUTRITIONAL INFO:
(PER SERVING)
CALORIES: 610
NET CARBS: 5 G
CARBS: 6 G
FAT: 39 G
PROTEIN: 49 G
FIBER: 1 G

This dish uses Burgundy wine, but feel free to substitute that with a good red of your choice—good being the operative word here.

1. Place the bacon in a Dutch oven and cook over medium heat until crispy, about 8 minutes. Transfer to a paper towel–lined to drain.

2. Season the beef with salt and pepper. Working in batches so as not to crowd the pot, place the beef in the Dutch oven and cook until browned all over. Remove from the pot and set aside.

3. Place the onions and butter in the pot and sauté until the onions start to brown, about 10 minutes. For a richer flavor you can cook the onions until they start to brown. Add the mushrooms, season with salt and the cayenne pepper, and then stir in the garlic. Cook until the mushrooms release their liquid and start to brown, about 8 minutes.

4. Stir in the red wine, bouillon, and Bouquet Garni. Return the beef and bacon to the pot, add water until it is covering the mixture in the pot, and bring to a boil. If a thicker stew is desired, add the xanthan gum. Cover the Dutch oven, reduce the heat to low, and cook for about 1½ hours, stirring occasionally.

5. When the beef is fork-tender, remove the Bouquet Garni and ladle the stew into bowls. Garnish each portion with chives and a dollop of sour cream.

7 oz. bacon, cubed

35 oz. chuck roast, cubed

Salt and pepper, to taste

5.3 oz. onions, chopped

1 tablespoon unsalted butter

14 oz. button mushrooms, chopped

¼ teaspoon cayenne pepper

4 garlic cloves, minced

1 cup red wine

1 cube of beef bouillon

1 Bouquet Garni (see sidebar)

1¼ cups water

¼ teaspoon xanthan gum (optional)

1 tablespoon finely chopped fresh chives, for garnish

Sour cream, for garnish

BEEF STROGANOFF

SERVINGS: 5
PREP TIME: 10 MINUTES
COOKING TIME: 40 MINUTES

NUTRITIONAL INFO:
(PER SERVING)
CALORIES: 590
NET CARBS: 6 G
CARBS: 7 G
FAT: 43 G
PROTEIN: 50 G
FIBER: 1 G

This dish fell out of favor during the fat-and-cholesterol paranoia of the '80s, but when made with top-notch ingredients, you'll see why so many have a soft spot for it.

1. Season the beef with salt and pepper. Place the olive oil in a Dutch oven and warm over medium heat. Working in batches so as not to crowd the pot, add the beef and cook until it is browned all over. Remove the beef from the Dutch oven and set aside.

2. Add the butter, onions, and mushrooms to the pot and sauté until the vegetables start to brown, about 8 minutes. Season with salt, pepper, paprika, and cayenne pepper, add the water, and return the beef to the pot.

3. Reduce the heat to medium-low, and cook until the beef is fork-tender and the liquid has reduced by half or more, about 1 hour.

4. Stir in the sour cream and heavy cream, ladle into warmed bowls, and garnish with chives.

28.2 oz. chuck roast, cut into long strips

Salt and pepper, to taste

1 tablespoon olive oil

1 tablespoon unsalted butter

3.5 oz. onions, sliced

7 oz. button mushrooms, sliced

1 teaspoon paprika

½ teaspoon cayenne pepper

2¼ cups water

2.7 oz. sour cream

1.75 oz. heavy cream

Fresh chives, finely chopped, for garnish

CHILI CON CARNE

SERVINGS: 4
PREP TIME: 10 MINUTES
COOKING TIME: 40 MINUTES

NUTRITIONAL INFO:
(PER SERVING)
CALORIES: 503
NET CARBS: 7 G
CARBS: 11 G
FAT: 32 G
PROTEIN: 39 G
FIBER: 4 G

This version includes bacon and spinach as a way to include fat and greens, but feel free to leave them out.

1. Place the olive oil and bacon in a Dutch oven and cook over medium heat until the bacon's fat starts to render. Add the onions and sauté until translucent, about 3 minutes.

2. Add the garlic and sauté until it starts to brown, about 2 minutes. Stir in the bell peppers and ground beef and season with the salt, black pepper, cayenne, cumin, and paprika. Cook, while using a wooden spoon to break up the ground beef, until it starts to brown, about 6 minutes.

3. Stir in the tomatoes, mushrooms, and spinach and cook until the spinach starts to wilt, about 2 minutes. Add the bouillon cube and water and cook until the liquid has reduced, about 10 minutes.

4. Add the fresh oregano and cilantro and cook until the chili has reduced to the desired consistency. Ladle into warmed bowls and serve with the sour cream and avocado.

1 tablespoon olive oil

7 oz. bacon, chopped

3.5 oz. onions, chopped

3 garlic cloves, minced

2.7 oz. green bell peppers, chopped

8.8 oz. ground beef

Salt, to taste

1 teaspoon black pepper

1 teaspoon cayenne pepper

1 teaspoon cumin

1 teaspoon paprika

7 oz. tomatoes, pureed

7 oz. button mushrooms, sliced

3.5 oz. spinach

1 cube of beef bouillon

2¼ cups water

Fresh oregano, finely chopped, to taste

Fresh cilantro, finely chopped, to taste

Sour cream, for serving

Avocado, chopped, for serving

COTTAGE PIE

SERVINGS: 5
PREP TIME: 10 MINUTES
COOKING TIME: 35 MINUTES

NUTRITIONAL INFO:
(PER SERVING)
CALORIES: 311
NET CARBS: 7 G
CARBS: 10 G
FAT: 16 G
PROTEIN: 30 G
FIBER: 3 G

Shepherd's pie is made with ground lamb. When it's made with ground beef, it becomes a cottage pie. This latter gets the keto makeover with—you guessed it—cauliflower taking the place of the potato.

1. Bring salted water to a boil in a large saucepan, add the cauliflower, and cook until tender, about 5 minutes. Drain, place the cauliflower in a food processor, and puree until smooth. Add the egg yolks and cheese, season with salt and pepper, and blitz to incorporate. Set the mixture aside.

2. Place the butter and olive oil in a skillet and warm over medium heat. When the butter starts to foam, add the onions and sauté until golden brown, about 10 minutes. Add the garlic and sauté until it starts to brown, about 1 minute. Add the ground beef and cook, while using a wooden spoon to break it up, until it has browned, about 8 minutes.

3. Preheat the oven to 390°F. Add the bouillon cube, Worcestershire sauce, tomato puree, rosemary, and thyme and cook, while stirring frequently, for 2 to 3 minutes.

4. Stir in the mushrooms and spinach, season to taste, and cook until the spinach has wilted, about 2 minutes. Add the water and cook until the liquid has reduced, about 10 minutes.

5. Place the ground beef mixture in a casserole dish, spread the cauliflower puree on top, sprinkle additional Parmesan over the cottage pie, and bake for about 15 minutes, until the top is golden brown. Remove and let cool slightly before serving.

Salt and pepper, to taste

17.6 oz. cauliflower, chopped

2 egg yolks

1.75 oz. Parmesan cheese, plus more to taste

2 tablespoons unsalted butter

1 tablespoon olive oil

1.75 oz. onions, chopped

4 garlic cloves, minced

17.6 oz. ground beef

1 cube of beef bouillon

1 teaspoon Worcestershire sauce

1.75 oz. tomato puree

½ tablespoon finely chopped fresh rosemary

½ tablespoon dried thyme

3.5 oz. button mushrooms, diced

3.5 oz. spinach

¾ cup water

WIENER SCHNITZEL

SERVINGS: 2
PREP TIME: 10 MINUTES
COOKING TIME: 10 MINUTES

NUTRITIONAL INFO: (PER SERVING)
CALORIES: 409
NET CARBS: 2 G
CARBS: 5 G
FAT: 25 G
PROTEIN: 39 G
FIBER: 3 G

The key is exercising patience when pounding the cutlets thin. Do that, and the rest of the preparation is effortless.

1. Place the Bread Crumbs, parsley, garlic powder, and Parmesan cheese in a bowl and stir to combine. Envelop the cutlets in plastic wrap and use a meat tenderizer to pound them as thin as possible. Season with salt and pepper.

2. Place the egg in a bowl and beat until scrambled. Dip the cutlets into the egg and then into the bread crumb mixture until coated.

3. Add olive oil or lard to a skillet until it is about 1 inch deep and warm over medium heat. Add the cutlets and fry until golden brown and cooked through, about 3 to 4 minutes. Drain on paper towel–lined plates, serve with mesclun greens, and garnish with the slices of lemon.

3.5 oz. Bread Crumbs (see page 53)

1 tablespoon finely chopped fresh parsley

1 teaspoon garlic powder

1 oz. Parmesan cheese, grated

9.1 oz. veal cutlets

Salt and pepper, to taste

1 egg

Olive oil or lard, as needed

Mesclun greens, for serving

2 lemon slices, for garnish

BACON BOMB BALLS

SERVINGS: 5
(1 SERVING = 1 BALL)
PREP TIME: 5 MINUTES
COOKING TIME: 20 MINUTES

NUTRITIONAL INFO:
(PER SERVING)
CALORIES: 330
NET CARBS: 1 G
CARBS: 1 G
FAT: 22 G
PROTEIN: 30 G
FIBER: 0 G

Packed with protein and fat, low on carbs, and bursting with flavor—these just may be the ideal snack for the keto disciple.

1. Preheat the oven to 400°F. Place the pork, garlic, rosemary, five-spice powder, cayenne pepper, salt, and pepper in a bowl in stir to combine. Divide the mixture into 1.75-oz. portions, place a cube of mozzarella on top of each, and form the portions into meatballs around the cheese.

2. Wrap each meatball with a strip of bacon, place them on a baking sheet, and cook in the oven for 20 minutes. Remove and garnish with grated Parmesan cheese and parsley.

8.8 oz. ground pork

2 garlic cloves, minced

1 teaspoon finely chopped fresh rosemary

½ teaspoon five-spice powder

½ teaspoon cayenne pepper

Salt and pepper, to taste

3.5 oz. mozzarella cheese, cubed

8.8 oz. bacon

Parmesan cheese, grated, for garnish

Fresh parsley, chopped, for garnish

BACON BOMB

SERVINGS: 5
PREP TIME: 40 MINUTES
COOKING TIME: 45 MINUTES

**NUTRITIONAL INFO:
(PER SERVING)**
CALORIES: 435
NET CARBS: 1 G
CARBS: 1 G
FAT: 36 G
PROTEIN: 26 G
FIBER: 0 G

This recipe is perfect for those who don't want to mess with a lot of prep, and it's also a great way to get in your protein and fat macros for the day. Plus, who can turn down this much bacon?

1. Season the pork with salt, pepper, paprika, cayenne pepper, and Italian seasoning. Place the mixture on a piece of plastic wrap and form it into a square. Place the cheese, scallion, and bell pepper in the center of the square.

2. Roll the meat into a thick log and refrigerate for 30 minutes, making sure it is rolled up tightly in the plastic wrap.

3. Preheat the oven to 390°F. Lay the strips of bacon on a piece of parchment paper. Remove the meat from the refrigerator and discard the plastic wrap. Place the log on top of the bacon and wrap the bacon around the roll.

4. Brush the log with some of the sauce, place it on a wire rack set in a baking sheet, and place in the oven. Bake for 20 minutes, baste with the remaining sauce, and return to the oven. Bake for another 25 minutes, remove from the oven, and let it rest for 15 minutes before serving.

17.6 oz. ground pork

Salt, to taste

½ tablespoon black pepper

1 tablespoon paprika

½ tablespoon cayenne pepper

2 tablespoons Italian seasoning

0.8 oz. cheddar cheese, grated

1 tablespoon chopped scallion

0.7 oz. bell pepper, diced

6 strips of bacon

3 tablespoons Barbecue Sauce (see page 71)

BARBECUE SPARERIBS

SERVINGS: 5
PREP TIME: 5 MINUTES
COOKING TIME: 35 MINUTES

NUTRITIONAL INFO:
(PER SERVING)
CALORIES: 569
NET CARBS: 1 G
CARBS: 1 G
FAT: 47 G
PROTEIN: 30 G
FIBER: 0 G

While some people might scoff at the idea of pressure-cooked ribs, once you see that meat fall off the bone and you taste that tangy sauce, you'll be giving this dish a thumbs up!

1. Place the spareribs, salt, cinnamon stick, bay leaf, peppercorns, star anise, garlic, and ginger in a pressure cooker and cook until tender, about 30 minutes.

2. Remove the ribs from the pressure cooker and place them in a bowl. Add the five-spice powder and sauce, season with salt, and stir to incorporate.

3. Place the ribs in a skillet and cook over medium-high heat until a crust forms on each side, 2 to 3 minutes per side. Serve immediately.

35.2 oz. pork spareribs

Salt, to taste

1 cinnamon stick

1 bay leaf

8 peppercorns

2 star anise pods

4 garlic cloves, minced

1 tablespoon minced ginger

1 tablespoon five-spice powder

¼ cup Barbecue Sauce (see page 71)

PORK CHOPS IN CREAMY MUSTARD SAUCE

SERVINGS: 4
PREP TIME: 5 MINUTES
COOKING TIME: 15 MINUTES

NUTRITIONAL INFO:
(PER SERVING)
CALORIES: 423
NET CARBS: 1 G
CARBS: 2 G
FAT: 30 G
PROTEIN: 33 G
FIBER: 1 G

The key to this dish is your timing while cooking the pork chops. Once you get that down, it'll become a weeknight staple.

1. Score the layer of fat on the outside of each pork chop with a knife. Season with salt, pepper, and the cayenne pepper.

2. Place the coconut oil in a skillet and warm over medium heat. When the oil starts to shimmer, add the pork chops and cook for 2 minutes per side (for average thickness). Turn chops so they are fat-side down and cook until the fat has rendered, another 2 minutes.

3. Lay the pork chops flat and stir in the butter, garlic, and rosemary. Cook, while basting the chops, until they are firm to the touch with a slight amount of spring. Remove from the pan and set aside.

4. Drain the excess fat from pan, add the bell pepper, and sauté until softened, about 5 minutes. Deglaze the pan with water and stir in the mustard and the resting juices from the pork chops.

5. Add the cream and cheese and cook, while stirring, until the cheese melts. Ladle the sauce over the pork chops, garnish with the scallion greens, and serve.

17.6 oz. pork chops

Salt and pepper, to taste

½ teaspoon cayenne pepper

1 tablespoon coconut oil

1 tablespoon unsalted butter

1 garlic clove, minced

1 sprig of fresh rosemary

1 green bell pepper, chopped

½ cup water

1 tablespoon mustard

3.5 oz. heavy cream

1.2 oz. cheddar cheese, grated

1 scallion green, chopped, for garnish

PORK CARNITAS

SERVINGS: 8
PREP TIME: 45 MINUTES
COOKING TIME: 4 HOURS

**NUTRITIONAL INFO:
(PER SERVING)**
CALORIES: 548
NET CARBS: 1 G
CARBS: 1 G
FAT: 40 G
PROTEIN: 44 G
FIBER: 0 G

The melt-in-your mouth pork that results makes this one well worth the time.

1. Preheat the oven to 285°F. Place the pork shoulder in a mixing bowl. Place the remaining ingredients in a separate bowl and stir until combined. Rub the seasoning mixture into the pork shoulder and let it sit for 30 minutes.

2. Place the pork shoulder in a roasting pan, cover it with aluminum foil, and roast for 3½ hours, until the pork shoulder is falling apart. Remove from the oven and pour the juices in the pan into a jar. The juices will separate into two layers—the top is fat and the bottom is jus.

3. Spoon some of the fat over pork. Turn the broiler on high and broil until the outside of the pork is crispy, about 15 minutes. Remove from the oven and serve immediately.

53-oz. boneless pork shoulder, cut into cubes

1 teaspoon kosher salt

1 teaspoon black pepper

1 teaspoon cumin

½ teaspoon five-spice powder

½ teaspoon cayenne pepper

2 cinnamon sticks, chopped

2 bay leaves

5 garlic cloves, minced

Zest and juice of 1 lemon

PULLED PORK

SERVINGS: 6

PREP TIME: 5 MINUTES

COOKING TIME:
2 HOURS AND 10 MINUTES

**NUTRITIONAL INFO:
(PER SERVING)**

CALORIES: 471

NET CARBS: 1 G

CARBS: 1 G

FAT: 34 G

PROTEIN: 39 G

FIBER: 0 G

One of the best things about keto is discovering that one can freely enjoy beloved dishes just like this one.

1. Preheat the oven to 300°F. Rub the pork shoulder with the olive oil. Place the remaining ingredients in a mixing bowl, stir to combine, and then rub the mixture all over the pork shoulder.

2. Place the pork shoulder on a rack set in a roasting pan. Fill the pan with water, cover the pan with aluminum foil, and roast for 2 hours, until the pork shoulder is extremely tender.

3. Remove the foil, raise the oven's temperature to 390°F, and return the pork shoulder to the oven. Cook for another 10 minutes, until the exterior is crispy. Remove from the oven, remove the bone from the pork shoulder, shred the meat with a fork, and serve.

35-oz. bone-in pork shoulder

1 tablespoon olive oil

2 teaspoons kosher salt

1 teaspoon black pepper

1 teaspoon paprika

1 teaspoon cayenne pepper

1 teaspoon garlic powder

½ teaspoon five-spice powder

½ teaspoon cinnamon

½ teaspoon stevia or preferred keto-friendly sweetener

PORK FRIED RICE

SERVINGS: 4
PREP TIME: 5 MINUTES
COOKING TIME: 20 MINUTES

NUTRITIONAL INFO:
(PER SERVING)
CALORIES: 274
NET CARBS: 6 G
CARBS: 11 G
FAT: 18 G
PROTEIN: 20 G
FIBER: 5 G

A fusion of Asian and Italian, this dish truly has it all.

1. Place the olive oil and butter in a large skillet and warm over medium heat. When the butter starts to foam, add the scallion whites and the ground pork and cook, while breaking the pork up with a fork, until the pork starts to brown, about 8 minutes.

2. Add the garlic, salt, pepper, paprika, cayenne pepper, oregano, red pepper flakes, bell peppers, and spinach and sauté until the spinach wilts, about 2 minutes.

3. Stir in the Cauliflower Rice, cheddar cheese, heavy cream, and scallion greens. Cook for 1 minute, stir in the olives, garnish with parsley and Parmesan, and serve.

1 tablespoon olive oil

1 tablespoon unsalted butter

1 scallion, trimmed and chopped, whites and greens separated

8.8 oz. ground pork

2 garlic cloves, chopped

1 teaspoon kosher salt

½ teaspoon black pepper

½ teaspoon paprika

¼ teaspoon cayenne pepper

1 teaspoon dried oregano

½ teaspoon red pepper flakes

3.5 oz. bell peppers, chopped

7 oz. baby spinach

17.6 oz. Cauliflower Rice (see page 214)

1.75 oz. cheddar cheese, grated

1 oz. heavy cream

8 olives, pitted and chopped

Fresh parsley, chopped, for garnish

Parmesan cheese, grated, for garnish

MEATZA

SERVINGS: 2
PREP TIME: 5 MINUTES
COOKING TIME: 20 MINUTES

**NUTRITIONAL INFO:
(PER SERVING)**
CALORIES: 417
NET CARBS: 1 G
CARBS: 2 G
FAT: 26 G
PROTEIN: 36 G
FIBER: 1 G

Using meat as the base takes pizza's few negatives and turns them into overwhelming positives.

1. Preheat the broiler to high. Place the ground meat in a bowl and season it with salt, pepper, and garlic powder. Stir to combine and set the mixture aside.

2. Place the olive oil in a cast-iron skillet and press the meat into the shape of a pizza that is about ½ inch thick. Cook over high heat until the meat is nearly cooked all the way through. Remove from heat, spread the pesto over the "pizza," and then top with the mushrooms, cheese, and pepperoni. Place the skillet under the broiler and broil for 10 minutes, until the cheese has melted and browned. Remove from the oven and serve immediately.

8.8 oz. ground chicken, beef, or pork

Salt and pepper, to taste

1 teaspoon garlic powder

1 teaspoon olive oil

1 tablespoon Basil Pesto (see page 72)

⅓ oz. mushrooms, sliced

2.6 oz. mozzarella cheese, grated

0.7 oz. pepperoni

COQ AU VIN

SERVINGS: 4
PREP TIME: 10 MINUTES
COOKING TIME: 35 MINUTES

NUTRITIONAL INFO: (PER SERVING)
CALORIES: 785
NET CARBS: 4 G
CARBS: 5 G
FAT: 64 G
PROTEIN: 61 G
FIBER: 1 G

The "coq" in this dish's name comes from the tradition of cooking roosters—these tough, old birds benefitted from the long braising and cooking time—but today almost everyone uses good ol' chicken.

1. Place the bacon in a skillet and cook over medium heat until it is crispy, about 8 minutes. Transfer to a paper towel–lined plate to drain.

2. Season the chicken legs with salt and pepper. Place them in the skillet and cook, while basting, until they are crispy and golden brown all over, about 5 minutes. Remove from the pan and set aside.

3. Place the mushrooms and onions in the skillet, season with salt and pepper, and sauté until the vegetables start to brown, about 8 minutes. Stir in the thyme and then deglaze the pan with the wine.

4. Return the chicken and half of the bacon to the pan, add the stock, cover the pan, and reduce the heat to medium-low. Cook until the chicken is tender and cooked through, about 15 minutes.

5. Remove the chicken from the pan and set aside. Raise the heat to medium-high and cook until the sauce has reduced to the desired consistency. Return the chicken to the pan, garnish with the remaining bacon and the parsley, and serve.

7 oz. bacon, cubed

4 bone-in, skin-on chicken legs

Salt and pepper, to taste

7 oz. white mushrooms, sliced

3.5 oz. pearl onions

3 sprigs of fresh thyme

5.3 oz. dry red wine

7 oz. chicken stock

Fresh parsley, finely chopped, for garnish

CREAMY CHICKEN CURRY

SERVINGS: 5
PREP TIME: 30 MINUTES
COOKING TIME: 30 MINUTES

NUTRITIONAL INFO:
(PER SERVING)
CALORIES: 290
NET CARBS: 3 G
CARBS: 3 G
FAT: 15 G
PROTEIN: 28 G
FIBER: 0 G

If you have time to spare, let the chicken marinate in the refrigerator for up to 8 hours and then let it come to room temperature before placing it in the pan.

1. Place the chicken pieces, half of the ginger and garlic, the lime juice, salt, red chili powder, turmeric, garam masala, and coriander in a bowl, and stir until the chicken is completely coated. Let the chicken marinate for 30 minutes.

2. Place half of the butter in a skillet and melt over medium heat. Add the onion, cumin, cloves, and cardamom and sauté until the onion turns translucent, about 3 minutes. Stir in the remaining ginger and garlic, as well as the almonds, and cook for 2 minutes.

3. Stir in the tomato puree and cook for 5 minutes, adding water as needed to prevent the mixture burning. Transfer the mixture to a blender and puree.

4. Place the remaining butter in the pan and melt over medium heat. Add the chicken pieces and cook until crispy, about 6 minutes. Deglaze the pan with the water, stir in the puree, and cover the pan. Reduce the heat to low and cook until the chicken is cooked through, about 10 minutes. Garnish with the cilantro and cream and serve immediately.

1 whole chicken, skin removed, cut into breasts, thighs, and drumsticks

1 teaspoon mashed ginger

1 teaspoon mashed garlic

½ tablespoon fresh lime juice

1 teaspoon kosher salt

1 teaspoon chili powder

1 teaspoon turmeric

½ teaspoon garam masala

1 teaspoon coriander

2 tablespoons unsalted butter

1.75 oz. onion, chopped

1 teaspoon cumin

3 whole cloves

3 cardamom pods

1 tablespoon chopped almonds

1.75 oz. tomato puree

¾ cup water, plus more as needed

6 tablespoons finely chopped fresh cilantro, for garnish

1.75 oz. heavy cream, for garnish

CHICKEN NUGGETS

SERVINGS: 8
(1 SERVING = 1 NUGGET)
PREP TIME: 10 MINUTES
COOKING TIME: 10 MINUTES

NUTRITIONAL INFO:
(PER SERVING)
CALORIES: 58
NET CARBS: 0 G
CARBS: 0 G
FAT: 3 G
PROTEIN: 8 G
FIBER: 0 G

You can use bread crumbs for these nuggets, but psyllium husk makes a perfect breading, and it will save you some precious calories.

1. Place the chicken, Old Bay Seasoning, salt, and pepper in a food processor and blitz until the mixture is almost a paste. Shape the mixture into nuggets, place them on a parchment-lined baking sheet, and refrigerate for 15 minutes.

2. Place the egg in a bowl, season with salt, and beat until combined. Place psyllium husk in another bowl. Dip a nugget into the egg and then into the psyllium husk. Repeat until all of the nuggets are completely coated.

3. Add lard or olive oil to a Dutch oven and heat it over medium-high heat. When it is about 350°F, add the chicken nuggets and cook, while turning, until the nuggets are cooked through. Place on paper towel–lined plates to drain before serving.

8.8 oz. boneless, skinless chicken breasts

1 teaspoon Old Bay Seasoning

Salt and pepper, to taste

1 egg

Psyllium husk, as needed

Lard or olive oil, as needed

CHICKEN SATAY WINGS

SERVINGS: 7
(1 SERVING = 1 FULL WING)
PREP TIME: 5 MINUTES
COOKING TIME: 25 MINUTES

**NUTRITIONAL INFO:
(PER SERVING)**
CALORIES: 103
NET CARBS: 2 G
CARBS: 2 G
FAT: 5 G
PROTEIN: 11 G
FIBER: 0 G

The ever-versatile chicken wing here takes on a Thai classic.

1. Place the peanut butter, coconut milk, soy sauce, vinegar, sriracha, fish sauce, salt, pepper, ginger, and garlic powder in a bowl and stir to combine. Add the chicken wings and toss until they are evenly coated. Let the mixture sit for 1 hour.

2. Preheat the oven to 410°F. Sprinkle the sesame seeds over the chicken wings, place them on a wire rack set in a baking sheet, and bake them for 25 minutes, until golden brown and cooked through. Remove from the oven and serve with hot sauce.

1 tablespoon natural, no sugar added peanut butter

1 oz. coconut cream

5 teaspoons soy sauce

1 tablespoon rice vinegar

2 teaspoons sriracha

2 teaspoons fish sauce

Salt and pepper, to taste

½ teaspoon ground ginger

½ teaspoon garlic powder

17.6 oz. chicken wings, separated into drumette and flat

¼ teaspoon black sesame seeds

¼ teaspoon white sesame seeds

Keto-friendly hot sauce, for serving

CREAM OF CHICKEN SOUP

SERVINGS: 4
PREP TIME: 5 MINUTES
COOKING TIME: 25 MINUTES

**NUTRITIONAL INFO:
(PER SERVING)**
CALORIES: 259
NET CARBS: 3 G
CARBS: 3 G
FAT: 20 G
PROTEIN: 15 G
FIBER: 0 G

The additional vegetables and seasonings take this soup to the next level, making it a winter staple.

1. Season the chicken with salt, pepper, dried oregano, and cayenne pepper and set it aside. Place the butter and olive oil in a saucepan and warm over medium heat. When the butter starts to foam, add the scallion whites and the celery and sauté until they start to soften, about 5 minutes.

2. Add the chicken, raise the heat to medium-high, and cook until browned, about 6 minutes. Stir in the garlic and scallion greens and cook until the garlic starts to brown, about 2 minutes.

3. Add the chicken stock and water, season to taste, and bring the soup to a gentle boil. Remove the pan from heat, stir in the cream and parsley, and serve immediately.

7 oz. boneless chicken, chopped

Salt, to taste

½ teaspoon black pepper

½ teaspoon dried oregano

¼ teaspoon cayenne pepper

3 tablespoons unsalted butter

1 tablespoon olive oil

1 scallion, whites and greens separated and chopped

0.7 oz. celery, chopped

3 garlic cloves, minced

17.6 oz. chicken stock

¾ cup water

3.5 oz. heavy cream

3 tablespoons finely chopped fresh parsley

CHICKEN PARMESAN

SERVINGS: 2
PREP TIME: 10 MINUTES
COOKING TIME: 20 MINUTES

**NUTRITIONAL INFO:
(PER SERVING)**
CALORIES: 477
NET CARBS: 3 G
CARBS: 4 G
FAT: 32 G
PROTEIN: 47 G
FIBER: 1 G

Coating the chicken with fresh parsley and Parmesan cheese not only saves calories, it adds flavor.

1. Preheat the broiler to high. Envelop the chicken breasts in plastic wrap and beat with a meat tenderizer until they are thin. Season with salt and pepper on both sides.

2. Place the egg and Italian seasoning in a bowl and stir to combine. Combine the Parmesan and parsley in another bowl. Dip the chicken into the egg mixture and then dip it into the Parmesan mixture until coated.

3. Place the olive oil and half of the butter in a skillet and warm over medium heat. When the butter starts to foam, add the chicken breasts and cook until browned and cooked through, about 1½ minutes per side. Remove from the pan and set aside.

4. Add the garlic to the skillet and cook until it starts to brown, about 2 minutes. Add the tomatoes, salt, oregano, red pepper flakes, and the remaining butter, cover the pan, and cook over medium heat for 4 to 5 minutes. Stir in the basil and remove the pan from heat.

5. Spread the tomato sauce in a baking dish, place the chicken on top, and top with mozzarella. Broil for 7 to 8 minutes, until the cheese is melted and browned.

10.6 boneless, skinless chicken breasts, butterflied

Salt and pepper, to taste

½ egg

1 teaspoon Italian seasoning

1 oz. Parmesan cheese, grated

1 tablespoon finely chopped fresh parsley

1 tablespoon olive oil

1 tablespoon unsalted butter

2 garlic cloves, minced

3.5 oz. tomatoes, pureed

1 teaspoon dried oregano

½ teaspoon red pepper flakes

1 tablespoon finely chopped fresh basil

3.5 oz. mozzarella cheese, grated

CHICKEN IN MUSHROOM SAUCE

SERVINGS: 4
PREP TIME: 10 MINUTES
COOKING TIME: 15 MINUTES

**NUTRITIONAL INFO:
(PER SERVING)**
CALORIES: 491
NET CARBS: 4 G
CARBS: 5 G
FAT: 28 G
PROTEIN: 41 G
FIBER: 1 G

Mushrooms and creamy sauces are a match made in keto heaven, and this savory dish is ideal for when you need a quick, comforting dinner.

1. Season the chicken breasts with salt, pepper, and paprika. Place the olive oil in a skillet and warm over high heat. When the oil starts to shimmer, add the chicken and cook until browned on each side, about 2 minutes per side. Remove from the pan and set aside.

2. Add the butter, mushrooms, thyme, and garlic, season with salt, and cook until the mushrooms release their liquid, about 3 minutes. Add the water and cheese and stir until melted. Stir in the cream and cook until the sauce reaches the desired consistency. Add the fresh parsley.

3. Slice the chicken breasts, pour the sauce over the top, and serve.

2 boneless, skinless chicken breasts, butterflied

Salt and pepper, to taste

¼ teaspoon paprika

1 tablespoon olive oil

1 tablespoon unsalted butter

3.5 oz. button mushrooms, chopped

Fresh thyme, finely chopped, to taste

2 garlic cloves, minced

¼ cup water

2.1 oz. Swiss cheese, grated

3.5 oz. heavy cream

Fresh parsley, finely chopped, to taste

CHICKEN THIGHS WITH MUSTARD GRAVY

SERVINGS: 2
PREP TIME: 5 MINUTES
COOKING TIME: 25 MINUTES

**NUTRITIONAL INFO:
(PER SERVING)**
CALORIES: 546
NET CARBS: 5 G
CARBS: 6 G
FAT: 41 G
PROTEIN: 39 G
FIBER: 1 G

Chicken skin is delicious and full of good fat, and it is nearly irresistible when paired with mustard gravy.

1. Season the chicken thighs with salt, pepper, and paprika.

2. Warm a cast-iron skillet over medium-high heat. Add the olive oil and place the chicken thighs skin-side down in the pan. Cook until the skin is crispy, 4 to 5 minutes, turn them over, and cook for an additional 2 minutes. Remove from the pan and set aside.

3. Add the butter and melt over medium heat. When the butter starts to foam, add the red onion and garlic and cook until the onion is translucent and starting to soften, about 5 minutes. Deglaze the pan with the vinegar and stock. Add the mustards and stir until a sauce begins to form.

4. Return the chicken to the pan, skin-side up, cover the pan, and cook until they are cooked through, about 8 minutes. Remove the chicken thighs, stir the cream and parsley into the sauce, and spoon it over the thighs.

4 skin-on, bone-in chicken thighs

½ teaspoon kosher salt

½ teaspoon black pepper

½ teaspoon smoked paprika

1 tablespoon olive oil

1 tablespoon unsalted butter

1 oz. red onion, chopped

4 garlic cloves, chopped

1 tablespoon white wine vinegar

3.5 oz. chicken stock

1 teaspoon whole-grain mustard

1 teaspoon Dijon mustard

1.75 oz. heavy cream

1 tablespoon finely chopped fresh parsley

LEMON-PEPPER CHICKEN

SERVINGS: 2
PREP TIME: 5 MINUTES
COOKING TIME: 15 MINUTES

**NUTRITIONAL INFO:
(PER SERVING)**
CALORIES: 426
NET CARBS: 1 G
CARBS: 1 G
FAT: 24 G
PROTEIN: 52 G
FIBER: 0 G

Outstanding flavor doesn't get any easier than lemon-pepper seasoning with some chicken, cheese, and cream.

1. Season the chicken with the lemon-pepper seasoning. Place the olive oil in a skillet and warm over medium heat. When the oil starts to shimmer, add the chicken and cook until golden brown all over, 3 to 4 minutes per side.

2. Deglaze the pan with the water. Add the cheese and cream and stir until the cheese is melted. Season with salt, stir in the chives and parsley, and serve.

10.6 oz. boneless, skinless chicken breasts

2 teaspoons lemon-pepper seasoning

1 tablespoon olive oil

¼ cup water

1.75 oz. cheddar cheese, grated

1.75 oz. heavy cream

Salt, to taste

1 teaspoon finely chopped fresh chives

1 teaspoon finely chopped fresh parsley

CREAMY PESTO CHICKEN

SERVINGS: 1
PREP TIME: 10 MINUTES
COOKING TIME: 10 MINUTES

NUTRITIONAL INFO:
(PER SERVING)
CALORIES: 563
NET CARBS: 2 G
CARBS: 2 G
FAT: 38 G
PROTEIN: 39 G
FIBER: 0 G

This is so simple to make that you won't quite believe how satisfied you feel after gobbling it down.

1. Envelop the chicken breast in plastic wrap and beat it with a meat tenderizer until it is thin. Season with salt and pepper on both sides.

2. Place the olive oil in a skillet and warm over high heat. When the oil starts to shimmer, add the chicken and cook for 2 minutes on each side. Remove from the pan and deglaze the pan with water. Stir in the pesto, cheese, and cream and cook until heated through. Add the resting juices from the chicken and stir to incorporate. Slice the chicken, pour the sauce over it, and serve.

1 boneless, skinless chicken breast

Salt and pepper, to taste

1 tablespoon olive oil

¼ cup water

1 tablespoon Basil Pesto (see page 72)

1 oz. Parmesan cheese, grated

1.75 oz. heavy cream

BACON-WRAPPED CHICKEN

SERVINGS: 2
PREP TIME: 5 MINUTES
COOKING TIME: 20 MINUTES

NUTRITIONAL INFO:
(PER SERVING)
CALORIES: 400
NET CARBS: 3 G
CARBS: 3 G
FAT: 22 G
PROTEIN: 49 G
FIBER: 0 G

After sitting in a luscious creamy marinade, this chicken doesn't need bacon wrapped around it—but it definitely doesn't hurt.

1. Separate the chicken legs into the drumstick and thigh and score the pieces with a knife.

2. Place the yogurt and cream cheese in a bowl and stir to combine. Add the remaining ingredients, except for the bacon, to the mixture and stir to combine. Place the chicken in the mixture and let it marinate for 1 hour.

3. Preheat the oven to 410°F. Wrap a strip of bacon around each piece of chicken, place them on a baking sheet, and bake in the oven for about 20 minutes, until the chicken is cooked through and the bacon crispy. Remove and let cool briefly before serving.

2 skinless chicken legs

2 tablespoons plain yogurt

1 tablespoon cream cheese

2 garlic cloves, minced

1 oz. mozzarella or cheddar cheese, grated

Cajun seasoning, to taste

Dried thyme, to taste

Black pepper, to taste

4 strips of bacon

CHICKEN & FALAFEL WRAPS

SERVINGS: 8
PREP TIME: 10 MINUTES
COOKING TIME: 1 HOUR AND 15 MINUTES

NUTRITIONAL INFO:
(PER SERVING)
CALORIES: 571
NET CARBS: 17.7 G
CARBS: 28.8 G
FAT: 39.1 G
PROTEIN: 29.9 G
FIBER: 11.1 G

You could enjoy both pieces of this on their own, but joining them in a wrap makes for a far more memorable experience.

1. Preheat the oven to 375°F. Pat the chicken dry and season the cavity with salt and pepper.

2. Place the butter, thyme, chili powder, salt, and pepper in a bowl and stir to combine. Rub the mixture over the exterior of the chicken. Place the garlic and lemon in the cavity.

3. Place the chicken in a roasting pan, place it in the oven, and roast for about 1 hour and 15 minutes, until the juices run clear when the thickest part of the thigh is pierced. The interior should register at least 165°F on an instant-read thermometer. While the chicken is roasting, baste it with its juices from time to time. Remove from the oven, cover with aluminum foil, and let it rest for about 10 minutes.

4. Whisk the olive oil and lemon juice together, season with salt and pepper, and then add the cabbages and carrots. Toss to combine and then serve the salad alongside the chicken, hummus, falafel, wraps, cucumbers, and oregano.

3-lb. chicken

¾ teaspoon kosher salt, plus more to taste

½ teaspoon black pepper, plus more to taste

4 tablespoons unsalted butter, at room temperature

Leaves from 4 sprigs of fresh thyme, chopped

1 teaspoon chili powder

1 head of garlic, halved

1 lemon, cut into wedges

¼ cup olive oil

2 tablespoons fresh lemon juice

2 large carrots, peeled and julienned

½ small red cabbage, shredded

¼ small white cabbage, shredded

Cauliflower Hummus (see page 80)

Zucchini Falafel (see page 200)

Keto Wraps (see page 46)

8 Persian cucumbers, sliced or quartered

1 oz. fresh oregano, chopped

POT STICKERS

SERVINGS: 5
(1 SERVING = 2 POT
STICKERS)
PREP TIME: 15 MINUTES
COOKING TIME: 25 MINUTES

**NUTRITIONAL INFO
FOR POT STICKERS:
(PER SERVING)**
CALORIES: 157
NET CARBS: 3 G
CARBS: 4 G
FAT: 7 G
PROTEIN: 21 G
FIBER: 1 G

These are delicious and can be customized to your taste, be it with a meat or vegetable filling.

1. Bring water to a boil in a large saucepan. Place the cabbage in the water and boil for 8 to 10 minutes. Combine the rest of the ingredients in a bowl and set it aside. Remove the cabbage and let cool. When the cabbage is cool enough to handle, peel off 10 full leaves.

2. Divide the chicken mixture into 1.75-oz. portions and place each one in a cabbage leaf. Wrap the leaf tightly around the filling to create a dumpling. Line a steaming tray with more cabbage leaves and place the dumplings in the tray.

3. Bring an inch of water to a boil in a saucepan. Place the steaming tray over the water and steam for about 10 minutes. Place the steamed dumplings in a skillet and cook over medium heat until browned on both sides, about 1 to 2 minutes per side. Serve with the Dipping Sauce.

1 cabbage

17.6 oz. ground chicken

0.8 oz. onion, grated

½ teaspoon mashed ginger

½ teaspoon mashed garlic

½ scallion, chopped

2 tablespoons finely chopped fresh cilantro

1 tablespoon sesame oil

Salt and pepper, to taste

Dipping Sauce (see sidebar), for serving

DIPPING SAUCE

Place 1 teaspoon natural, no sugar added peanut butter, 1 teaspoon sriracha, 1 teaspoon olive oil, ½ teaspoon soy sauce, ½ teaspoon rice vinegar, the juice of ½ lime, ¼ teaspoon mashed ginger, and ¼ teaspoon mashed garlic in a mixing bowl, season with salt, and stir until thoroughly combined. This recipe will make 2 servings of sauce; the macros per serving are as follows: 43 calories, 2 grams net carbs, 2 grams carbs, 4 grams fat, 1 gram protein, and 0 grams fiber.

FRIED CHICKEN

SERVINGS: 4
PREP TIME: 10 MINUTES
COOKING TIME: 10 MINUTES

**NUTRITIONAL INFO:
(PER SERVING)**
CALORIES: 358
NET CARBS: 1 G
CARBS: 2 G
FAT: 20 G
PROTEIN: 43 G
FIBER: 1 G

Usually, fried chicken comes with as much guilt as grease. But if you give it a keto-accommodating breading, all of that negative stuff evaporates.

1. Place the salt, pepper, paprika, cayenne pepper, and garlic powder in a bowl and stir to combine. Dredge the chicken breasts in the mixture until they are coated on both sides.

2. Place the egg in a bowl and beat until it is scrambled. Place the Bread Crumbs in another bowl. Dip each breast into the egg and then into the Bread Crumbs until coated.

3. Add your preferred cooking fat to a Dutch oven until it is 2 inches deep and bring to 350°F. Add the chicken and fry until golden brown and the chicken is cooked through, 3 to 4 minutes. Drain briefly on a paper towel–lined plate before serving.

1 teaspoon kosher salt

1 teaspoon black pepper

1 teaspoon smoked paprika

½ teaspoon cayenne pepper

1 teaspoon garlic powder

4 boneless, skinless chicken breasts

1 egg

3.5 oz. Bread Crumbs (see page 53)

Preferred cooking fat, as needed

BUFFALO WINGS

SERVINGS: 15
(1 SERVING = 1 FULL WING)
PREP TIME: 15 MINUTES
COOKING TIME: 25 MINUTES

NUTRITIONAL INFO:
(PER SERVING)
CALORIES: 166
NET CARBS: 0 G
CARBS: 0 G
FAT: 9 G
PROTEIN: 20 G
FIBER: 0 G

Of course, a keto version of these beloved wings had to happen, and these may be even better than the standard-bearers.

1. Preheat the oven to 400°F. Place the salt, pepper, paprika, and half of the hot sauce in a bowl and stir to combine. Add the chicken wings and let them marinate for about 10 minutes.

2. Place the wings on a wire rack set in a baking sheet. Place in the oven and bake for about 25 minutes, until the wings are cooked through. Remove from the oven and let them cool slightly.

3. Place the butter and cream cheese in a microwave-safe bowl and microwave for about 30 seconds, until the butter is completely melted. Add the remaining hot sauce to the mixture and stir until thoroughly combined. Toss the wings in the sauce and serve immediately.

1 teaspoon kosher salt

1 teaspoon black pepper

1 teaspoon paprika

3.5 oz. keto-friendly hot sauce

2¼ lbs. chicken wings, separated into drumette and flat

1.75 oz. unsalted butter

0.8 oz. cream cheese

GARLIC & PARMESAN CHICKEN WINGS

SERVINGS: 9
(1 SERVING = 1 FULL WING)
PREP TIME: 10 MINUTES
COOKING TIME: 35 MINUTES

NUTRITIONAL INFO:
(PER SERVING)
CALORIES: 263
NET CARBS: 1 G
CARBS: 1 G
FAT: 12 G
PROTEIN: 35 G
FIBER: 0 G

Use a quality good Parmesan cheese to make these, because it makes a huge difference in the flavor.

1. Preheat the oven to 375°F. Toss the wings in a bowl with the salt, pepper, cayenne, paprika, oregano, butter, and lemon juice. Place the wings on a wire rack set in a baking sheet, place them in the oven, and bake for 20 minutes, until they are golden brown. Remove the wings and increase the oven temperature to 400°F.

2. Combine the remaining ingredients in a bowl and then toss the chicken wings in the mixture. Place them back on the baking sheet and bake for another 10 minutes. Remove from the oven and serve immediately.

9 chicken wings, separated into drumette and flat

1 teaspoon kosher salt

½ teaspoon black pepper

½ teaspoon cayenne pepper

1 teaspoon smoked paprika

1 teaspoon dried oregano

1 tablespoon unsalted butter, melted

1 teaspoon fresh lemon juice

1 tablespoon hot sauce

4 garlic cloves, minced

1 teaspoon finely chopped fresh parsley

1.75 oz. Parmesan cheese, grated

GARLIC BUTTER SHRIMP

SERVINGS: 1
PREP TIME: 35 MINUTES
COOKING TIME: 5 MINUTES

NUTRITIONAL INFO:
(PER SERVING)
CALORIES: 452
NET CARBS: 3 G
CARBS: 5 G
FAT: 39 G
PROTEIN: 23 G
FIBER: 2 G

So good, it will have you licking the plate clean.

1. Place the shrimp, salt, pepper, cayenne, and oregano in a bowl and toss to combine. Refrigerate for 30 minutes.

2. Warm the olive oil and 1 tablespoon of the butter in a skillet. When the butter starts to foam, add the garlic and the parsley. Cook for 2 minutes and then add the shrimp. Cook until they are opaque, about 4 minutes. Remove the pan from heat and stir in the remaining butter and the lemon juice. Serve immediately.

3.5 oz. shrimp

¼ teaspoon kosher salt

¼ teaspoon black pepper

¼ teaspoon cayenne pepper

½ teaspoon dried oregano

1 tablespoon olive oil

2 tablespoons unsalted butter

2 garlic cloves, minced

1 tablespoon finely chopped fresh parsley

Juice of ½ lemon

GARLIC BUTTER CALAMARI

SERVINGS: 2
PREP TIME: 5 MINUTES
COOKING TIME: 5 MINUTES

NUTRITIONAL INFO:
(PER SERVING)
CALORIES: 271
NET CARBS: 7 G
CARBS: 7 G
FAT: 22 G
PROTEIN: 21 G
FIBER: 0 G

Quick to whip up and even easier to fall in love with, the results here are always impressive.

1. Season the squid with salt and pepper and set it aside. Place the butter in a skillet and melt it over medium heat. Add the garlic, parsley, cilantro, and scallion and cook over medium heat until the garlic starts to brown, about 2 minutes.

2. Raise the heat to high and add the calamari. Cook, stirring frequently, until the squid is just cooked through, 2 to 3 minutes. Stir in the Parmesan and lemon juice and serve.

   Tip: Squid cooks very quickly, so if there is a lot of liquid in the pan, remove the squid, cook down the liquid and, once it's almost gone, return the squid to the pan, turn off the heat, and finish the dish.

8.8 oz. calamari rings

Salt and pepper, to taste

1.75 oz. salted butter

5 garlic cloves, minced

Pinch of finely chopped fresh parsley

Pinch of finely chopped fresh cilantro

1 tablespoon minced scallion

1 teaspoon grated Parmesan cheese

Juice of 1 lemon wedge

FISH CAKES

SERVINGS: 6
(1 SERVING = 1 FISH CAKE)
PREP TIME: 5 MINUTES
COOKING TIME: 20 MINUTES

**NUTRITIONAL INFO:
(PER SERVING)**
CALORIES: 149
NET CARBS: 1 G
CARBS: 1 G
FAT: 9 G
PROTEIN: 15 G
FIBER: 0 G

Team these with some Mug Bread (see page 45) to make a fish sandwich.

1. Place all of the ingredients, except for the eggs and butter, in a mixing bowl and stir to combine. Incorporate the eggs and then form the mixture into six cakes.

2. Place the butter in a nonstick skillet and warm over medium heat. Working in batches, add the fish cakes and cook until browned and cooked through, about 3 to 4 minutes per side.

8.4 oz. canned tuna or salmon, drained

1 oz. red onion, diced

Leaves from 3 sprigs of fresh parsley, chopped

1 tablespoon mayonnaise

1 teaspoon mustard

1 teaspoon keto-friendly hot sauce

½ teaspoon garlic powder

½ teaspoon paprika

1.75 oz. Bread Crumbs (see page 53)

Salt and pepper, to taste

2 eggs

1 tablespoon unsalted butter

SALMON IN LEMON & CAPER BUTTER SAUCE

SERVINGS: 2
PREP TIME: 5 MINUTES
COOKING TIME: 15 MINUTES

NUTRITIONAL INFO:
(PER SERVING)
CALORIES: 392
NET CARBS: 7 G
CARBS: 9 G
FAT: 32 G
PROTEIN: 18 G
FIBER: 2 G

This recipe celebrates the process of acclimating to the ketogenic diet—the move from "fat is bad" to reveling in the innate goodness of butter.

1. Place the olive oil in a skillet and warm over medium heat. Season the salmon with salt and pepper. When the oil starts to shimmer, add the salmon and cook until it is cooked through, about 3 minutes per side. Remove from the pan and set aside.

2. Add the onions to the pan and cook until translucent, about 3 minutes. Reduce the heat to low and add half of the butter. When the butter has stopped foaming, stir in the garlic and capers and cook for 1 minute.

3. Turn off the heat and stir in the remaining butter, the parsley, and the lemon juice. Pour the pan sauce over the fish and serve.

1 tablespoon olive oil

Salt and pepper, to taste

8.8 oz. salmon fillets

1.75 oz. small red onions, chopped

2.8 oz. unsalted butter

4 garlic cloves, minced

1¾ tablespoons capers

1 tablespoon finely chopped fresh parsley

Fresh lemon juice, to taste

SHRIMP RISOTTO

SERVINGS: 2
PREP TIME: 5 MINUTES
COOKING TIME: 15 MINUTES

**NUTRITIONAL INFO:
(PER SERVING)**
CALORIES: 470
NET CARBS: 8 G
CARBS: 13 G
FAT: 36 G
PROTEIN: 31 G
FIBER: 5 G

Common culinary thinking holds that mixing dairy and seafood is a no-no, but this faux risotto proves to be the exception to the rule.

1. Place 1 tablespoon of the olive oil in a skillet and warm over medium-high heat. When the oil starts to shimmer, add the mushrooms and cook until they are browned, about 8 minutes. Remove from the pan and set aside.

2. Place the remaining olive oil and the butter in the skillet. Add the Cauliflower Rice, season with salt and pepper, and cook for 4 minutes, stirring constantly. Add the stock and cook for another 4 minutes. Season with the oregano and red pepper flakes.

3. Add the shrimp and cook for another 2 minutes, until the cauliflower is tender and the shrimp are cooked through. Remove the pan from heat and stir in the mascarpone cheese, mushrooms, and basil. Serve immediately.

2 tablespoons olive oil

3.5 oz. oyster or porcini mushrooms, chopped

1 tablespoon unsalted butter

10.6 oz. Cauliflower Rice (see page 214)

Salt and pepper, to taste

5.3 oz. fish stock

1 teaspoon dried oregano

½ teaspoon red pepper flakes

8.8 oz. shrimp

3.5 oz. mascarpone cheese

1 tablespoon finely chopped fresh basil

SEAFOOD SALAD

SERVINGS: 1
PREP TIME: 10 MINUTES
COOKING TIME: 10 MINUTES

NUTRITIONAL INFO:
(PER SERVING)
CALORIES: 574
NET CARBS: 7 G
CARBS: 9 G
FAT: 42 G
PROTEIN: 38 G
FIBER: 2 G

The butter-poached shrimp, soft-boiled eggs, and lettuce create a salad that you absolutely don't want to miss.

1. Place the onion and the lemon juice in a bowl, stir to combine, and set it aside. Place the butter in a saucepan and melt over the lowest heat possible. Add the garlic, salt, pepper, and dried herbs and cook until the butter starts to foam. Add the shrimp and cook, while spooning the butter over them, until cooked through, about 3 minutes.

2. Remove the shrimp and garlic with a slotted spoon, grate the garlic, and place them in a bowl. Stir the mayonnaise, sriracha, and the butter into the pan and then add the dill. Stir to incorporate and set it aside.

3. Place the marinated onion, lettuce, black olives, gherkins, and soft-boiled egg in a bowl and toss to distribute. Top with the shrimp-and-garlic dressing, toss to combine, and serve.

0.8 oz. red onion, sliced

2 to 3 drops of fresh lemon juice

2 tablespoons salted butter

2 whole garlic cloves

Salt and pepper, to taste

3 tablespoons mixed dried herbs

10.6 oz. shrimp, shelled and deveined

1 tablespoon mayonnaise

1½ teaspoons sriracha

Fresh dill, finely chopped, to taste

3.5 oz. mesclun greens

1 oz. pitted black olives, chopped

1 oz. gherkins, chopped

1 soft-boiled egg, halved

TUNA SALAD

SERVINGS: 4
PREP TIME: 5 MINUTES
COOKING TIME: 10 MINUTES

**NUTRITIONAL INFO:
(PER SERVING)**
CALORIES: 326
NET CARBS: 0 G
CARBS: 6 G
FAT: 25 G
PROTEIN: 22 G
FIBER: 6 G

A slight twist on the standard, with bacon being added. After all, what salad is complete without it?

1. Place the cabbage, half of the mayonnaise and horseradish sauce, and the bacon in a bowl, season with salt and pepper, stir to combine, and set aside.

2. Chop two of the eggs, place them in a bowl, add the tuna, and stir to combine. Add the rest of the ingredients, along with the remaining mayonnaise and horseradish sauce, and stir to combine. Incorporate the cabbage mixture, cut the remaining eggs in half, and place them on top of each portion.

3.5 oz. cabbage, julienned

¼ cup mayonnaise

2 tablespoons horseradish sauce

2 strips of bacon, cooked and chopped

Salt and pepper, to taste

4 hard-boiled eggs

7 oz. canned tuna, drained

0.7 oz. celery, diced

0.7 oz. scallions, diced

0.7 oz. lettuce, diced

0.7 oz. green bell pepper, diced

1 teaspoon mustard

1 teaspoon sriracha

SPAGHETTI & MEATBALLS

**SERVINGS
(SQUID AND SAUCE):** 2

SERVINGS (MEATBALLS): 10 (1
SERVING = 1 MEATBALL)

PREP TIME: 15 MINUTES

COOKING TIME: 30 MINUTES

**NUTRITIONAL INFO:
(PER SERVING OF
SPAGHETTI)**

CALORIES: 206

NET CARBS: 6 G

CARBS: 7 G

FAT: 14 G

PROTEIN: 13 G

FIBER: 1 G

**NUTRITIONAL INFO:
(PER MEATBALL)**

CALORIES: 139

NET CARBS: 0 G

CARBS: 0 G

FAT: 10 G

PROTEIN: 11 G

FIBER: 0 G

Zucchini noodles are wonderful, but it is inevitable that you'll eventually get tired of them. When that moment arrives, here's another lovely pasta alternative.

FOR THE MEATBALLS

8.8 oz. ground beef

8.8 oz. ground pork

1 oz. Parmesan cheese, grated

½ oz. cheddar cheese, grated

1 tablespoon finely chopped
fresh parsley

1 teaspoon finely chopped fresh
thyme

1 teaspoon garlic powder

½ teaspoon cayenne pepper

½ teaspoon black pepper

1 teaspoon kosher salt

1 egg

1 tablespoon olive oil

FOR THE SPAGHETTI & SAUCE

1 tablespoon unsalted butter

1 tablespoon olive oil

2.1 oz. button mushrooms, chopped

1 teaspoon kosher salt

½ teaspoon black pepper

½ teaspoon red pepper flakes

1 teaspoon dried oregano

3.5 oz. tomatoes

¼ cup water

5.3 oz. squid, cut into long strips

1 tablespoon finely chopped
fresh basil

1. To prepare the meatballs, place all of the ingredients, except for the olive oil, in a mixing bowl and stir until thoroughly combined. Form the mixture into golf ball–sized spheres. Place the olive oil in a skillet and warm over medium heat. When the oil starts to shimmer, add the meatballs to the skillet in batches and cook, while turning, until they are browned all over and cooked through. Transfer the cooked meatballs to a bowl and tent with aluminum foil to keep warm.

2. To begin preparations for the spaghetti and sauce, place the butter and olive oil in the skillet and warm over medium heat. Add the mushrooms and cook until they start to brown, about 8 minutes. Season with the salt, pepper, red pepper flakes, and oregano.

3. Stir in the tomatoes and water, cover the pan, and cook until the sauce has reduced slightly, 5 to 7 minutes. Season with salt, add the squid, and cook until just cooked through, about 2 minutes. Stir in the basil and serve alongside the meatballs.

DEVILED EGGS

SERVINGS: 6
PREP TIME: 10 MINUTES
COOKING TIME: 10 MINUTES

**NUTRITIONAL INFO:
(PER SERVING)**

CALORIES: 202

NET CARBS: 3.6 G

CARBS: 4 G

FAT: 13.8 G

PROTEIN: 13.2 G

FIBER: 0.4 G

Back after briefly becoming a punch line, these make for a perfect lunch or midday snack.

1. Place the eggs in a large saucepan and cover by 2 inches with cold water. Bring to a boil, reduce the heat, and steadily simmer for 10 minutes. Drain and rinse the eggs under cold water for 2 minutes.

2. Crack and peel the eggs, rinsing off any shell. Carefully slice the eggs in half, remove the yolks, and place them in a mixing bowl. Mash the yolks with a fork and reserve the halved egg whites.

3. Add the mayonnaise, mustard, capers, caper brine, sun-dried tomatoes, olive oil, salt, and pepper to the mashed yolks and stir until thoroughly combined. Spoon the mixture into the egg white halves and garnish with parsley.

12 large eggs

½ cup mayonnaise

2 teaspoons Dijon mustard

1 tablespoon capers, chopped, plus 1 teaspoon caper brine

2 tablespoons chopped sun-dried tomatoes

1 tablespoon olive oil

½ teaspoon kosher salt

¼ teaspoon black pepper

¼ cup fresh parsley, torn

EAT YOUR VEGGIES

With keto, most of the emphasis is placed on making sure you get enough protein and fat, and that you maintain a watchful eye for carbs. This latter charge means that vegetables, which can be rife with those pests, take more of a back seat than they do in most diets. But they are still an important source of vitamins and fiber, both of which are a must if you are going to lose weight at your optimal rate. And they are still delicious. This collection of entrees, sides, soups, and salads will help you out the next time you need to go green.

CAULIFLOWER MASH

SERVINGS: 4
PREP TIME: 5 MINUTES
COOKING TIME: 10 MINUTES

**NUTRITIONAL INFO:
(PER SERVING)**
CALORIES: 162
NET CARBS: 3 G
CARBS: 6 G
FAT: 15 G
PROTEIN: 3 G
FIBER: 3 G

The versatility of cauliflower was unknown until keto came along. Here, it takes the form of a creamy mash, so perfect in texture and taste, you'll never guess it's not a potato.

1. Bring salted water to a boil in a saucepan and add the cauliflower. Cook until tender, about 7 minutes, and drain.

2. Place the cauliflower, butter, cream, salt, and pepper in a food processor and blitz until the mixture is a rich, smooth paste. Serve immediately.

Salt and pepper, to taste

8 oz. cauliflower florets

1.75 oz. unsalted butter

1.75 oz. heavy cream

EGGPLANT PARMESAN

SERVINGS: 4
PREP TIME: 10 MINUTES
COOKING TIME: 30 MINUTES

NUTRITIONAL INFO: (PER SERVING)
CALORIES: 241
NET CARBS: 5 G
CARBS: 9 G
FAT: 18 G
PROTEIN: 14 G
FIBER: 4 G

This Italian classic is so decadent that you don't even notice the lack of meat in it.

1. Preheat the oven to 390°F. Place the eggplant in a colander, season it with salt, and let it sit for 30 minutes.

2. Pat the eggplant dry. Coat the bottom of a skillet with olive oil and warm over medium heat. When the oil starts to shimmer, add the eggplant in batches and cook until browned on each side. Set the cooked slices of eggplant on a paper towel–lined plate to drain.

3. Spread some of the sauce in a baking or gratin dish. Sprinkle some of the Parmesan on top, and then layer some eggplant on top. Repeat this layering process until all of the components have been used. Place the dish in the oven and bake for about 15 minutes until the cheese is melted and golden brown. Remove from the oven, garnish with basil, and serve.

10.6 oz. eggplant, sliced

Salt, to taste

Olive oil, as needed

7 oz. Marinara Sauce (see page 75)

1.75 oz. Parmesan cheese, grated

1.75 oz. mozzarella cheese, grated

Fresh basil, for garnish

CHEESY BACON SLAW

SERVINGS: 2
PREP TIME: 5 MINUTES
COOKING TIME: 10 MINUTES

NUTRITIONAL INFO:
(PER SERVING)
CALORIES: 328
NET CARBS: 3 G
CARBS: 5 G
FAT: 29 G
PROTEIN: 14 G
FIBER: 2 G

This warm slaw is packed with flavor, and it's a fantastic way to sneak some vegetables and fiber into your diet.

1. Place the bacon in a skillet and cook over medium heat until it is crispy, about 8 minutes.

2. Add the cabbage to the pan and season the mixture with salt, pepper, paprika, and dried oregano. As the cabbage starts to soften, stir in the cheese and cream. When the cabbage is cooked to your liking, remove the pan from heat, garnish with fresh parsley, and serve.

3.5 oz. bacon, chopped

5.3 oz. cabbage, shredded

Salt and pepper, to taste

¼ teaspoon paprika

½ teaspoon dried oregano

1 oz. cheddar cheese, grated

1.75 oz. heavy cream

Fresh parsley, finely chopped, for garnish

CREAMED SPINACH

SERVINGS: 1
PREP TIME: 2 MINUTES
COOKING TIME: 5 MINUTES

**NUTRITIONAL INFO:
(PER SERVING)**
CALORIES: 283
NET CARBS: 2 G
CARBS: 4 G
FAT: 26 G
PROTEIN: 9 G
FIBER: 2 G

Perfect on the side with a well-seared steak or a piece of roast chicken, this is another great way to get your greens.

1. Place the olive oil in a skillet and warm over medium heat. When the oil starts to shimmer, add the spinach, season with salt, pepper, and the nutmeg, and cook until the spinach has wilted, about 2 minutes.

2. Stir in the butter, cheese, and cream and cook for 1 minute before serving.

1 tablespoon olive oil

3.5 oz. spinach

Salt and pepper, to taste

⅛ teaspoon ground nutmeg

2 teaspoons unsalted butter

0.7 oz. Parmesan cheese, grated

2 tablespoons heavy cream

SAUTÉED MUSHROOMS

SERVINGS: 1
PREP TIME: 5 MINUTES
COOKING TIME: 5 MINUTES

**NUTRITIONAL INFO:
(PER SERVING)**
CALORIES: 250
NET CARBS: 5 G
CARBS: 7 G
FAT: 22 G
PROTEIN: 10 G
FIBER: 2 G

These are great on top of a burger as a condiment, and also a midafternoon snack.

1. Place the oil in a skillet and warm over medium-high heat. When the oil starts to shimmer, add the mushrooms, season with salt and pepper, and then stir in half of the butter and the rosemary. Cook until the mushrooms release their liquid, about 3 minutes.

2. Add the garlic and sauté until the mushrooms are browned, about 7 minutes. Remove the pan from heat, stir in the remaining butter, and serve immediately.

1 tablespoon olive oil

3.5 oz. button mushrooms, sliced

1.75 oz. oyster mushrooms, chopped

Salt and pepper, to taste

1 tablespoon unsalted butter

1 sprig of fresh rosemary

1 garlic clove, minced

SOUR CREAM & BACON CAULIFLOWER TART

SERVINGS: 8
PREP TIME: 10 MINUTES
COOKING TIME: 50 MINUTES

NUTRITIONAL INFO:
(PER SERVING)
CALORIES: 373
NET CARBS: 14.5 G
CARBS: 20.7 G
FAT: 26.3 G
PROTEIN: 15.8 G
FIBER: 6.2 G

Tangy sour cream and the do-everything flavor of bacon make each bite of this tart something to savor.

---

8 oz. cauliflower florets

Pinch of kosher salt, plus more to taste

1 egg, beaten

⅓ cup goat cheese, at room temperature

2 tablespoons cornstarch

2 tablespoons olive oil

1 cup sour cream

6 strips of bacon, chopped

1 red onion, sliced thin

Black pepper, to taste

1. Preheat the oven to 400°F. Line a large baking sheet with parchment paper and spray it with nonstick cooking spray. Bring salted water to a boil in a large saucepan. Place the cauliflower florets in a food processor and pulse until they are rice-like in texture. Add them to the boiling water, cover the pan, and cook until tender, 4 to 5 minutes.

2. Drain and place the cauliflower in a kitchen towel. Wring the towel to remove as much liquid as possible and then place the cauliflower in a bowl. Add the egg, goat cheese, and cornstarch, season with salt, and stir until the mixture just starts holding together.

3. Place the mixture on the baking sheet and shape it into a large oval. Brush the top with the olive oil, place it in the oven, and bake for about 35 minutes, until the top is golden brown and dry to the touch. Remove from the oven, spread the sour cream over the tart, and sprinkle the bacon on top. Return to the oven and bake for about 10 minutes, until the bacon is crispy. Remove from the oven, top with the onion, and season with salt and pepper. Let the tart cool briefly before serving.

EDAMAME FALAFEL

SERVINGS: 6
PREP TIME: 10 MINUTES
COOKING TIME: 30 MINUTES

NUTRITIONAL INFO: (PER SERVING)
CALORIES: 230
NET CARBS: 9.4 G
CARBS: 13.4 G
FAT: 15.7 G
PROTEIN: 11 G
FIBER: 4 G

Baking the falafel instead of frying it makes for a much lighter preparation, meaning you can easily afford to pair this with your favorite dip.

1. Preheat the oven to 400°F. Place the garlic, scallion, and herbs in a food processor and pulse until the mixture is finely chopped. Add all of the remaining ingredients, except for the sunflower seeds and olive oil, and blitz until the mixture is almost smooth. Add the sunflower seeds and pulse to incorporate.

2. Grease a large, rimmed baking sheet with 1 tablespoon of the oil. Scoop 1½-tablespoon portions of the mixture onto the baking sheet and brush each one with the remaining oil. Place in the oven and bake until the falafels are golden brown, about 30 minutes. Remove from the oven and let cool for 5 minutes before serving.

2 garlic cloves, crushed

1 scallion, trimmed and chopped

2 oz. fresh parsley, torn

2 oz. fresh cilantro, torn

17.6 oz. shelled edamame

Flesh of 1 small avocado

¼ cup almond meal

½ teaspoon cumin

½ teaspoon coriander

¼ teaspoon baking powder

1 teaspoon kosher salt

½ teaspoon black pepper

2 tablespoons fresh lemon juice

2 tablespoons sunflower seeds

2 tablespoons olive oil

CAULIFLOWER FRITTERS

SERVINGS: 4
PREP TIME: 5 MINUTES
COOKING TIME: 30 MINUTES

**NUTRITIONAL INFO:
(PER SERVING)**
CALORIES: 560
NET CARBS: 8.4 G
CARBS: 15.6 G
FAT: 51.1 G
PROTEIN: 11.2 G
FIBER: 7.2 G

The malleable flavor of cauliflower is the perfect canvas for the unique zing of basil.

1. To begin preparation for the fritters, bring two inches of water to a simmer in a saucepan. Place the cauliflower florets in a food processor and blitz until they are rice-like in consistency. Place in a steaming tray and steam until the cauliflower is just tender, 3 to 4 minutes. Transfer the cauliflower to a large mixing bowl and let it cool for 5 minutes.

2. Add the cream cheese, the 2 tablespoons of coconut flour, flaxseed meal, eggs, dried basil, salt, and pepper to the bowl and stir until combined. Scoop the mixture onto parchment-lined baking sheets and press down on them until they are flat. Place in the refrigerator for 30 minutes.

3. Dust the fritters with the remaining coconut flour and then shake off any excess. Place the oil in a large skillet and warm it over medium heat. Working in batches of three or four, place the fritters in the oil and fry until golden brown all over, about 3 minutes per side. Place the cooked fritters on a paper towel–lined plate and tent with aluminum foil to keep warm.

4. To prepare the dip, place all of the ingredients in a bowl and stir to combine. Serve alongside the fritters.

FOR THE FRITTERS

6.5 oz. cauliflower florets

⅓ cup cream cheese, at room temperature

2 tablespoons coconut flour, plus ¼ cup

2 tablespoons flaxseed meal

2 large eggs, lightly beaten

1 teaspoon dried basil

½ teaspoon kosher salt

¼ teaspoon black pepper

⅓ cup avocado oil

FOR THE DIP

⅓ cup mayonnaise

⅓ cup plain Greek yogurt

⅓ cup cream cheese, at room temperature

2 tablespoons finely chopped fresh basil

¼ teaspoon kosher salt

¼ teaspoon black pepper

¼ cup warm water (110°F)

CAULIFLOWER PIZZA

SERVINGS: 1
PREP TIME: 10 MINUTES
COOKING TIME: 35 MINUTES

NUTRITIONAL INFO:
(PER SERVING)
CALORIES: 301
NET CARBS: 8 G
CARBS: 14 G
FAT: 18 G
PROTEIN: 22 G
FIBER: 6 G

Discovering that you can eat pizza on keto is enough to get many to try the diet out. Discovering this particular pizza is what keeps many of those people committed to it.

1. Preheat the oven to 375°F and line a baking sheet with parchment paper. Place the cauliflower florets in a food processor and blitz until they are the consistency of couscous. Place the cauliflower in a dry skillet and cook over medium heat until browned and tender, 5 to 6 minutes. Place the cauliflower in a kitchen towel, wring it to remove as much water as possible, and place it in a mixing bowl.

2. Season the cauliflower with salt and pepper, add the cream cheese, Parmesan, and egg, and stir to combine. Place the mixture on the baking sheet and shape it into a circle. Place it in the oven and bake for 20 minutes.

3. Remove from the oven and turn the "crust" over. Spread the sauce over it and distribute the mozzarella and salami on top. Return to the oven and bake for about 15 minutes, until the cheese is melted and starting to brown. Remove from the oven and let cool briefly before serving.

8.8 oz. cauliflower florets

Salt and pepper, to taste

½ oz. cream cheese

1 oz. Parmesan cheese, grated

1 egg

2 tablespoons Marinara Sauce (see page 75)

1.75 oz. mozzarella cheese, grated

1 oz. salami, sliced thin

CAULIFLOWER MAC & CHEESE

SERVINGS: 4
PREP TIME: 10 MINUTES
COOKING TIME: 35 MINUTES

NUTRITIONAL INFO:
(PER SERVING)
CALORIES: 481
NET CARBS: 9 G
CARBS: 12 G
FAT: 43 G
PROTEIN: 17 G
FIBER: 3 G

Yes, it's technically cauliflower and cheese, but by now you should know that cauliflower is whatever you want it to be.

1. Preheat the oven to 390°F. Place the unsalted butter in a skillet and melt over medium heat. Add the onion and garlic and sauté until the onion is translucent, about 3 minutes. Stir in the ham and red pepper flakes and sauté until the ham starts to brown, about 5 minutes. Remove the pan from heat.

2. Season the cauliflower florets with salt and microwave for 5 minutes, until tender.

3. Place the salted butter in a saucepan and melt over medium heat. Stir in the garlic powder, cayenne, pepper, nutmeg, thyme, and bouillon cube. When the butter stops foaming, add the cream and cook, while stirring constantly, until the liquid has reduced by one-quarter. Stir in two-thirds of the cheese and cook until it has melted. Season with pepper and remove the pan from heat.

4. Place the cauliflower, ham-and-onion mixture, and cheese sauce in a bowl and stir to combine. Transfer the mixture to a casserole dish and top with pine nuts and the remaining cheese.

5. Place in the oven and bake for 10 to 12 minutes. Turn on the broiler and broil until the top is crispy and golden brown, about 2 minutes. Remove from the oven and serve.

1 teaspoon unsalted butter

1 small onion, chopped

½ garlic clove, minced

3.5 oz. ham, chopped

½ teaspoon red pepper flakes

17.6 oz. cauliflower florets

Salt, to taste

1.75 oz. salted butter

½ teaspoon garlic powder

½ teaspoon cayenne pepper

½ teaspoon grated fresh nutmeg

1 teaspoon finely chopped fresh thyme

½ cube of chicken bouillon

10.6 oz. heavy cream

5.3 oz. cheddar cheese, grated

Black pepper, to taste

0.8 oz. pine nuts, crushed

MINI VEGGIE PIZZAS

SERVINGS: 4
PREP TIME: 5 MINUTES
COOKING TIME: 40 MINUTES

**NUTRITIONAL INFO:
(PER SERVING)**
CALORIES: 185
NET CARBS: 7.2 G
CARBS: 10.3 G
FAT: 13.4 G
PROTEIN: 7.9 G
FIBER: 3.1 G

These pizzas prove once again that roasting vegetables in the oven is often the best route to maximizing your own enjoyment.

1. Preheat the oven to 400°F. Place the squash, zucchini, and eggplant on a large, rimmed baking sheet, pat dry with paper towels, season with salt, and let them sit for 15 minutes. Brush with the olive oil, place them in the oven, and roast for about 20 minutes, until they start to brown.

2. Remove the vegetables from oven and top each one with some of the tomatoes, onion, and mozzarella. Sprinkle the salt and pepper on top, return them to the oven, and bake for about 15 minutes, until the cheese has melted. Remove from the oven and let cool briefly before serving.

½ yellow squash, sliced ½ inch thick

½ zucchini, sliced ½ inch thick

½ eggplant, sliced ½ inch thick

1 teaspoon kosher salt, plus more to taste

2 tablespoons olive oil

2 vine tomatoes, sliced

½ red onion, sliced

1 cup shredded mozzarella cheese

¼ teaspoon black pepper

CREAM OF MUSHROOM SOUP

SERVINGS: 3
PREP TIME: 5 MINUTES
COOKING TIME: 25 MINUTES

NUTRITIONAL INFO:
(PER SERVING)
CALORIES: 230
NET CARBS: 6 G
CARBS: 8 G
FAT: 21 G
PROTEIN: 4 G
FIBER: 2 G

The key to avoiding the famously bland taste of the canned variety is cooking the mushrooms until all of their liquid has evaporated, concentrating the flavor.

2 tablespoons olive oil

3 tablespoons unsalted butter

4 garlic cloves, minced

4.4 oz. button mushrooms, stems chopped and caps sliced

4.4 oz. portobello mushrooms, stems chopped and caps sliced

1 cube of chicken or vegetable bouillon

½ teaspoon kosher salt

½ teaspoon black pepper

¼ teaspoon cayenne pepper

½ teaspoon paprika

1¼ cups water

3.5 oz. heavy cream

3.5 oz. oyster mushrooms, chopped

1 tablespoon Parmesan cheese, for garnish (1 teaspoon per serving)

Fresh basil, finely chopped, for garnish

1. Place 1 tablespoon of the olive oil and 1 tablespoon of the butter in a saucepan and warm over medium heat. When the butter starts to foam, add the garlic and cook until it starts to brown, about 2 minutes. Add the mushroom stalks and a handful of the sliced mushroom caps, the bouillon cube, and half of the salt, pepper, and cayenne. Stir in the paprika and cook until all of the liquid from the mushrooms has evaporated and they are well browned, about 8 minutes.

2. Add the water and cook for 2 minutes. Place the mixture in a blender or food processor and puree until smooth. Set the mixture aside.

3. Place 1 tablespoon of the butter in the pan and melt it over medium heat. Add the remaining mushroom caps and cook until all of their liquid has evaporated, about 8 minutes. Strain the puree into the saucepan and bring the mixture to a simmer.

4. Stir in the cream, reduce the heat to low, and let the mixture simmer gently for 6 minutes. Remove the soup from heat.

5. Place the oyster mushrooms in a skillet with the remaining butter, olive oil, salt, pepper, and cayenne and sauté until they are well browned and crispy, about 12 minutes. Ladle the soup into bowls and top each portion with the sautéed oyster mushrooms, cheese, and fresh basil.

BROCCOLI & CHEDDAR SOUP

SERVINGS: 4
PREP TIME: 5 MINUTES
COOKING TIME: 20 MINUTES

NUTRITIONAL INFO: (PER SERVING)
CALORIES: 356
NET CARBS: 8 G
CARBS: 12 G
FAT: 30 G
PROTEIN: 10 G
FIBER: 4 G

Good luck finding another soup that combines cheese and veggies so deliciously.

1. Place the olive oil and 1 tablespoon of the butter in a saucepan and warm over medium heat. When the butter starts to foam, add the onion and broccoli stalks and cook until the onion starts to brown, about 6 minutes.

2. Stir in the garlic, season with salt, pepper, paprika, and cayenne, and cook for 1 minute. Deglaze the pan with the stock or water, cover the pan, and cook for 5 minutes.

3. Transfer the contents of the saucepan to a food processor or blender and puree until smooth and creamy. Set aside.

4. Place the remaining butter in the saucepan and melt over medium heat. Add the broccoli florets and cook, without stirring, until they are seared, about 3 minutes. Strain the puree into the saucepan and bring the soup to a boil. Reduce heat so that the soup simmers and cook for 5 minutes.

5. Stir in the cream and the cheese and cook until all the cheese has melted. Serve immediately.

1 tablespoon olive oil

3 tablespoons unsalted butter

1.75 oz. onion, chopped

17.6 oz. broccoli, stalks chopped, florets diced

4 garlic cloves, minced

Salt, to taste

½ teaspoon black pepper

1 teaspoon paprika

½ teaspoon cayenne pepper

2¼ cups chicken stock or water

5.3 oz. heavy cream

3.5 oz. cheddar cheese, grated

SPINACH SOUP

SERVINGS: 2
PREP TIME: 5 MINUTES
COOKING TIME: 15 MINUTES

NUTRITIONAL INFO:
(PER SERVING)
CALORIES: 216
NET CARBS: 7 G
CARBS: 9 G
FAT: 19 G
PROTEIN: 4 G
FIBER: 2 G

This creamy and rich soup will quickly become a favorite way to get your greens on keto.

1. Place the butter in a saucepan and melt over medium heat. Add the onion and sauté until translucent, about 3 minutes. Stir in the garlic and cook until it starts to brown, about 2 minutes.

2. Add the spinach, bouillon cube, and half of the water, cover the pan, and cook until the spinach wilts, about 3 minutes. Transfer the mixture to a blender or food processor and puree until smooth. Strain the soup back into the saucepan, add the remaining water, and bring it to a gentle simmer.

3. Stir in the cream and cook until the soup has reduced to the desired consistency. Season with pepper and ladle into warmed bowls.

1 tablespoon unsalted butter

3.5 oz. onion, chopped

4 garlic cloves, chopped

5.3 oz. spinach

1 cube of chicken bouillon

1¼ cups water

3.5 oz. heavy cream

Black pepper, to taste

TOMATO SOUP

SERVINGS: 3
PREP TIME: 5 MINUTES
COOKING TIME: 25 MINUTES

**NUTRITIONAL INFO:
(PER SERVING)**
CALORIES: 266
NET CARBS: 5 G
CARBS: 7 G
FAT: 26 G
PROTEIN: 2 G
FIBER: 2 G

This light, comforting soup will charge you with festive feelings thanks to the pumpkin spice.

1. Place the butter in a saucepan and melt over medium heat. Add the onion, season with salt, and sauté until the onion starts to turn brown and caramelize, about 6 minutes.

2. Stir in the garlic and cook until it starts to brown, about 2 minutes. Add the tomatoes, cook for 2 minutes, and cover the pan. Reduce the heat to low and cook for 5 minutes. If the mixture starts to look dry, add some water to the pan.

3. Stir in the black pepper, paprika, pumpkin spice, and stock. Cover the pan and cook for about 10 minutes, stirring occasionally.

4. Transfer the mixture to a blender or food processor and puree until smooth. Strain the soup back into the saucepan, stir in the cream, and cook over low heat until warmed through. Ladle into warmed bowls, season with salt and pepper, and garnish with the basil and Parmesan.

1.75 oz. salted butter

1.75 oz. onion, chopped

Salt, to taste

4 garlic cloves, chopped

10.6 oz. tomatoes, chopped

Water, as needed

½ teaspoon black pepper, plus more to taste

½ teaspoon smoked paprika

1 teaspoon pumpkin spice

3.5 oz. chicken stock, plus more as needed

3.5 oz. heavy cream

Fresh basil, finely chopped, for garnish

Parmesan cheese, grated, for garnish

ASIAN BEEF SALAD

SERVINGS: 1
PREP TIME: 5 MINUTES
COOKING TIME: 15 MINUTES

**NUTRITIONAL INFO:
(PER SERVING)**
CALORIES: 300
NET CARBS: 2.5 G
CARBS: 4 G
FAT: 22.5 G
PROTEIN: 21.5 G
FIBER: 1.5 G

Enoki mushrooms are recommended here because they create a noodle-like texture, but you can use any mushroom you like.

FOR THE DRESSING

2 tablespoons olive oil

1 tablespoon natural, no sugar added peanut butter

1 garlic clove, minced

1 teaspoon low-carb soy sauce

1 teaspoon white vinegar

Dash of fish sauce

Juice of 1 lime wedge

2 drops of stevia

Salt and pepper, to taste

FOR THE SALAD

10.6 oz. beef, sliced into thin strips

Salt, to taste

Curry powder, to taste

1 tablespoon olive oil

1 tablespoon unsalted butter

3.5 oz. enoki mushrooms, chopped

3.5 oz. mesclun greens

Fresh cilantro, finely chopped, for garnish

1 teaspoon sesame seeds, for garnish

1. To prepare the dressing, place all of the ingredients in a bowl and whisk until they are emulsified. Set aside.

2. To begin preparations for the salad, season the beef with salt and curry powder. Place the olive oil in a skillet and warm over medium-high heat. When the oil starts to shimmer, add the beef and cook until it is done to your liking. Remove from the pan and place it in a salad bowl.

3. Place the butter and mushrooms in the skillet, season with salt, and sauté until all of the liquid has evaporated. Add the mixture to the salad bowl along with the greens and dressing, toss to combine, and garnish with the cilantro and sesame seeds.

KALE CRISPS

SERVINGS: 4
PREP TIME: 5 MINUTES
COOKING TIME: 25 MINUTES

**NUTRITIONAL INFO:
(PER SERVING)**
CALORIES: 83
NET CARBS: 2.2 G
CARBS: 3.5 G
FAT: 7.3 G
PROTEIN: 1.2 G
FIBER: 1.3 G

A delicious preparation that makes incorporating this superfood into your diet a cinch.

1. Preheat the oven to 225°F. Rinse the kale and pat it dry with paper towels. Tear the leaves into large pieces, making sure to remove any thick stems. Place the kale in a mixing bowl, add the oil and salt, and toss until the kale is evenly coated.

2. Place the kale leaves on two baking sheets, place them in the oven, and bake for 15 minutes. Rotate the baking sheets and bake for another 10 minutes, until the kale is crispy. Remove from the oven and let cool briefly before serving.

7 oz. kale leaves

2 tablespoons olive oil

1 teaspoon flaky sea salt

VEGETARIAN SANDWICHES

SERVINGS: 4
PREP TIME: 5 MINUTES
COOKING TIME: 10 MINUTES

NUTRITIONAL INFO:
(PER SERVING)
CALORIES: 465
NET CARBS: 6.2 G
CARBS: 8.7 G
FAT: 44.1 G
PROTEIN: 10.7 G
FIBER: 2.5 G

If you're in need of some protein, some crispy bacon would fit nicely on this sandwich.

---

1. Place half of the olive oil in a skillet and warm over medium heat. When the oil starts to shimmer, add the mushrooms, onion, and peppers, season with salt, and sauté until all the vegetables start to soften, about 5 minutes. Add the spinach and cook until it has wilted, about 2 minutes. Remove the pan from heat.

2. Preheat the broiler to high. Brush the remaining olive oil on both sides of the slices of bread. Place the bread on a baking sheet, place them under the broiler, and broil until the tops are golden brown, 2 to 3 minutes. Remove from the oven and let them cool.

3. Place the mayonnaise and mustard in a small bowl and stir to combine. Spread the mixture on the untoasted sides of four slices of the bread. Arrange the peppers, spinach, red onion, and mushrooms, and microgreens on top of the spread, and assemble the sandwiches.

¼ cup olive oil

3.75 oz. mushrooms, sliced

1 small red onion, sliced

2 small red bell peppers, cored, seeded, and chopped

Salt, to taste

4 oz. baby spinach

8 slices of Cloud Bread (see page 50)

½ cup mayonnaise

1½ teaspoons Dijon mustard

½ cup microgreens

GO FOR THE GREEN

SERVINGS: 4
PREP TIME: 10 MINUTES
COOKING TIME: 10 MINUTES

**NUTRITIONAL INFO:
(PER SERVING)**
CALORIES: 325
NET CARBS: 5.5 G
CARBS: 10.2 G
FAT: 25.8 G
PROTEIN: 13.7 G
FIBER: 4.7 G

A sandwich that positively screams health. It's also quite satisfying, and surprisingly rich.

1. Preheat the broiler to high. Brush the olive oil on both sides of the slices of bread. Place the bread on a baking sheet, place them under the broiler, and broil until they are golden brown, 2 to 3 minutes. Remove from the oven and let them cool.

2. Spread the pesto on the untoasted sides of the bread. Top with the tomatoes, avocado, spinach, and feta and assemble the sandwiches with the other pieces of bread.

2 tablespoons olive oil

8 slices of Cloud Bread (see page 50)

6 tablespoons Basil Pesto (see page 72)

7 oz. cherry tomatoes, halved

Flesh of 1 large avocado, sliced

2 oz. baby spinach

½ cup crumbled feta cheese

ZUCCHINI FALAFEL

SERVINGS: 8
PREP TIME: 5 MINUTES
COOKING TIME: 20 MINUTES

**NUTRITIONAL INFO:
(PER SERVING)**
CALORIES: 282
NET CARBS: 6.9 G
CARBS: 10.5 G
FAT: 27 G
PROTEIN: 2.8 G
FIBER: 3.6 G

Adding zucchini to this Middle Eastern delicacy grants it a lightness that makes it an ideal snack.

1. Place the chickpeas, zucchini, garlic, and herbs in a food processor and pulse until the mixture is a rough puree. Transfer to a mixing bowl, add the baking powder and coconut flour, and work the mixture with your hands until it is a non-sticky dough. Add more coconut flour as needed if the dough is not quite holding together. Season with salt and pepper, form the dough into golf ball–sized spheres, and set them aside.

2. Place the oil in a Dutch oven and warm it to 350°F. Working in batches of three or four, add the falafel to the oil and fry until they are golden brown, 3 to 4 minutes. Place the cooked falafel on a paper towel–lined plate and tent with aluminum foil to keep warm.

7 oz. dried chickpeas, soaked overnight and drained

1 small zucchini, grated

2 garlic cloves, minced

8 oz. fresh parsley, finely chopped

4 oz. fresh cilantro, finely chopped

1½ teaspoons baking powder

3 tablespoons coconut flour, plus more as needed

Salt and pepper, to taste

4 cups vegetable oil

CHICKEN SALAD

SERVINGS: 2
PREP TIME: 10 MINUTES
COOKING TIME: 10 MINUTES

NUTRITIONAL INFO:
(PER SERVING)
CALORIES: 442
NET CARBS: 5 G
CARBS: 6 G
FAT: 35 G
PROTEIN: 27 G
FIBER: 1 G

This salad is refreshing with a creamy, yogurt-based dressing that helps you hit your fat macros but doesn't feel as heavy and oily as a mayo-based dressing would.

1. To begin preparations for the salad, place the chicken, salt, pepper, dried herbs, apple cider vinegar, and half of the olive oil in a bowl, stir to combine, and let the mixture sit for at least 30 minutes.

2. Place the remaining oil in a skillet and warm over medium heat. When the oil starts to shimmer, add the chicken and butter and cook until the chicken is cooked through, 2 to 3 minutes per side. Frequently baste the chicken with the melted butter as it cooks. Remove the chicken from the pan and set it aside.

3. To prepare the dressing, place all of the ingredients in a mixing bowl and stir until thoroughly combined.

4. Place the vegetables in a bowl and toss until evenly distributed. Slice the chicken, place it on top of the salad, and then sprinkle the feta over everything. Drizzle the dressing on top and serve.

FOR THE SALAD

6.2 oz. boneless chicken thighs

Salt, to taste

½ teaspoon black pepper

1 teaspoon dried herbs

½ tablespoon apple cider vinegar

1 tablespoon olive oil

½ tablespoon unsalted butter

3.5 oz. lettuce, sliced

1.75 oz. tomato, sliced

3.5 oz. cucumber, sliced

1 oz. pitted olives, sliced

1.75 oz. feta cheese, crumbled

FOR THE DRESSING

1 tablespoon full-fat Greek yogurt

2 tablespoons olive oil

1 teaspoon fresh lime or lemon juice

Juices from cooked chicken

Salt and pepper, to taste

½ teaspoon cayenne pepper

PESTO CHICKEN SALAD

SERVINGS: 2
PREP TIME: 20 MINUTES
COOKING TIME: 10 MINUTES

NUTRITIONAL INFO:
(PER SERVING)
CALORIES: 409
NET CARBS: 2 G
CARBS: 3 G
FAT: 32 G
PROTEIN: 28 G
FIBER: 1 G

The pesto and mozzarella take the standard chicken salad up a notch.

1. To begin preparations for the salad, place the chicken thighs in a bowl with the Italian seasoning, salt, and olive oil, toss until the chicken is coated, and let marinate for 10 minutes. Place the pine nuts in a dry skillet and toast over medium heat until they are browned, about 2 minutes. Transfer to a salad bowl and let cool.

2. Place the bacon fat in the skillet and warm over medium heat. When it is hot, add the chicken and cook until it is cooked through, 3 to 4 minutes per side. Remove from the pan and slice the chicken into strips.

3. To prepare the dressing, place all of the ingredients in a small bowl and stir to combine.

4. Add the chicken, greens, tomatoes, and mozzarella to the salad bowl and toss to combine. Drizzle the dressing over the top and serve.

FOR THE SALAD

5.3 oz. boneless chicken thighs

1 teaspoon Italian seasoning blend

Salt, to taste

1 teaspoon olive oil

½ oz. pine nuts

1 tablespoon bacon fat

3.5 oz. mesclun greens

1.75 oz. cherry tomatoes, halved

3.5 oz. fresh mozzarella cheese, torn

FOR THE DRESSING

1 tablespoon Basil Pesto (see page 72)

2 tablespoons mayonnaise

Juices from cooked chicken

BAKED ZUCCHINI CASSEROLE

SERVINGS: 1
PREP TIME: 10 MINUTES
COOKING TIME: 10 MINUTES

NUTRITIONAL INFO:
(PER SERVING)
CALORIES: 516
NET CARBS: 4 G
CARBS: 6 G
FAT: 46 G
PROTEIN: 20 G
FIBER: 2 G

This is arguably one of the easiest casserole recipes ever, and a great way to use some of the surplus of zucchini that every summer seems to bring.

1. Preheat the oven to 390°F. Place the zucchini, sauce, salami, and olive oil in a baking dish and stir to combine. Sprinkle the cheese over the mixture.

2. Place in the oven and bake for 10 minutes, until the cheese is golden brown. Remove from the oven and let cool briefly before serving.

3.5 oz. zucchini noodles

2.1 oz. Marinara Sauce (see page 75)

1 oz. salami

1 tablespoon olive oil

1.75 oz. mozzarella cheese, grated

FETTUCCINI ALFREDO

SERVINGS: 1
PREP TIME: 5 MINUTES
COOKING TIME: 10 MINUTES

NUTRITIONAL INFO:
(PER SERVING)
CALORIES: 426
NET CARBS: 7 G
CARBS: 8 G
FAT: 38 G
PROTEIN: 15 G
FIBER: 1 G

The rich, creamy flavor beloved by all, now without so many of those dastardly carbs.

1. Place the olive oil in a skillet and warm over medium-high heat. When the oil starts to shimmer, add the mushrooms and garlic and cook until the mushrooms start to brown, about 8 minutes. Add the zucchini and cook for a minute.

2. Stir in the cheese and cream and cook until the sauce starts to thicken. Season with salt and pepper and garnish with the bacon and parsley.

1 tablespoon olive oil

2 mushrooms, chopped

2 garlic cloves, pressed

3.5 oz. zucchini noodles

1 oz. Parmesan cheese, grated

1 oz. heavy cream

½ teaspoon kosher salt

½ teaspoon black pepper

2 thin strips of bacon, cooked and chopped, for garnish

Fresh parsley, finely chopped, for garnish

MUSHROOM RISOTTO

SERVINGS: 2
PREP TIME: 5 MINUTES
COOKING TIME: 10 MINUTES

**NUTRITIONAL INFO:
(PER SERVING)**
CALORIES: 263
NET CARBS: 7 G
CARBS: 11 G
FAT: 20 G
PROTEIN: 13 G
FIBER: 4 G

The cauliflower rice serves as a milky backdrop to all the wonderful flavors, giving this dish the feel of a true risotto.

1. Place the butter in a skillet and melt over medium heat. Add the garlic, season with pepper, and cook until the garlic starts to brown, about 2 minutes.

2. Add mushrooms and cook until they begin to brown, about 8 minutes. Stir in the Cauliflower Rice, Parmesan, and cream and cook until warmed through, about 2 minutes. Garnish with the parsley and serve.

1 tablespoon unsalted butter

4 garlic cloves, minced

Salt and pepper, to taste

3.5 oz. mushrooms, sliced

8.8 oz. Cauliflower Rice (see page 214)

1.75 oz. Parmesan cheese, grated

1.75 oz. heavy cream

1 teaspoon finely chopped fresh parsley, for garnish

SPAGHETTI WITH PESTO

SERVINGS: 1
PREP TIME: 5 MINUTES
COOKING TIME: 5 MINUTES

NUTRITIONAL INFO:
(PER SERVING)
CALORIES: 356
NET CARBS: 2 G
CARBS: 3 G
FAT: 35 G
PROTEIN: 8 G
FIBER: 1 G

This is the easiest and fastest dish you'll ever make. The best part is there is zero compromise on the flavor thanks to the pesto.

1. Place the olive oil in a skillet and warm over medium-high heat. When the oil starts to shimmer, add the zucchini noodles and cook until tender, about 5 minutes.

2. Stir in the pesto and cheese and cook until warmed through. Remove the pan from heat, garnish with additional Parmesan and pine nuts, and serve.

1 tablespoon olive oil

3.5 oz. zucchini noodles

1 tablespoon Basil Pesto (see page 72)

0.7 oz. Parmesan cheese, grated, plus more for garnish

0.7 oz. pine nuts, for garnish

CAULIFLOWER RICE

Making cauliflower rice is extremely simple. Cut 1 large head of cauliflower into chunks, place them in a food processor, and blitz until rice-like in consistency. Warm 1 tablespoon of olive oil in a skillet, add the cauliflower, and cook until it is tender, 4 to 5 minutes.

CHORIZO PILAF

SERVINGS: 2
PREP TIME: 5 MINUTES
COOKING TIME: 15 MINUTES

NUTRITIONAL INFO:
(PER SERVING)
CALORIES: 206
NET CARBS: 6 G
CARBS: 10 G
FAT: 16 G
PROTEIN: 6 G
FIBER: 4 G

Another spot where cauliflower's myriad talents step in to fill a massive void.

1. Place the olive oil in a skillet and warm over medium heat. When the oil starts to shimmer, add the chorizo and cook until it starts to brown, about 5 minutes. Add the cumin seeds, onion, ginger, and garlic and cook until the onion is soft, about 8 minutes.

2. Add the tomato, turmeric, paprika, and a splash of water and cook for 3 to 4 minutes. Season with salt and add another splash of water. Cook until the sauce has a gravy-like consistency.

3. Stir in the Cauliflower Rice and cook until all of the liquid has evaporated. Garnish with the cilantro and serve.

1 tablespoon olive oil

1.75 oz. chorizo, diced

½ teaspoon cumin seeds

1 oz. onion, chopped

½ teaspoon mashed ginger

½ teaspoon mashed garlic

1.75 oz. tomato, chopped

½ teaspoon turmeric

½ teaspoon sweet paprika

Salt, to taste

8.8 oz. Cauliflower Rice (see sidebar)

Fresh cilantro, finely chopped, for garnish

ZUCCHINI ROLLUPS

SERVINGS: 4
PREP TIME: 5 MINUTES
COOKING TIME: 20 MINUTES

NUTRITIONAL INFO:
(PER SERVING)
CALORIES: 337
NET CARBS: 2.1 G
CARBS: 2.7 G
FAT: 26.3 G
PROTEIN: 21.7 G
FIBER: 0.6 G

These rollups are fun, flavorful, and refreshing–exactly what you need in that limbo between lunch and dinner.

1. Pat the zucchini dry with paper towels, place them on a baking sheet, and brush them with 2 tablespoons of the olive oil. Place the zucchini in the oven and broil until they are browned on both sides, about 10 minutes. Remove from the oven and let cool.

2. Place the remaining oil in a skillet and warm it over medium heat. Add the fennel seeds and cook, while stirring, for 30 seconds. Add the pork, raise the heat to medium-high, and cook, while breaking up the pork with a fork, until it is starting to brown, about 6 minutes.

3. Stir in the shallot and garlic, reduce the heat to medium, and cook for 3 minutes. Remove the pan from heat and stir in the feta, salt, and pepper. Spoon the mixture over the slices of zucchini, roll them up, and secure with toothpicks.

2 zucchini, sliced very thin lengthwise

3 tablespoons olive oil

1 teaspoon fennel seeds

1 lb. ground pork

1 shallot, minced

2 garlic cloves, minced

1 oz. feta cheese, crumbled

¾ teaspoon kosher salt

¼ teaspoon black pepper

GRILLED ASPARAGUS WITH EGG SAUCE

SERVINGS: 4
PREP TIME: 5 MINUTES
COOKING TIME: 20 MINUTES

NUTRITIONAL INFO:
(PER SERVING)
CALORIES: 281
NET CARBS: 3.7 G
CARBS: 4.9 G
FAT: 28.6 G
PROTEIN: 2.6 G
FIBER: 1.2 G

The king of spring—asparagus—needs nothing. But with this rich egg sauce it becomes positively divine.

1. Bring water to a boil in a saucepan and prepare an ice water bath. Add the asparagus to the boiling water and cook until just tender to the tip of a knife, about 2 minutes. Transfer to the ice water bath, let sit for 2 minutes, and then drain. Pat the asparagus dry with paper towels and set aside.

2. Place the yogurt, mayonnaise, lemon juice, salt, pepper, and water in a bowl and stir to combine. Fold about half of the chopped eggs into the sauce and sprinkle the remaining chopped eggs and parsley on top.

3. Place the olive oil in a skillet and warm over high heat. When the oil starts to shimmer, add the asparagus and cook, while stirring, until it starts to brown all over, about 2 minutes. Serve alongside the sauce.

12 asparagus spears, trimmed

½ cup plain Greek yogurt

½ cup mayonnaise

2 tablespoons fresh lemon juice

½ teaspoon kosher salt

⅛ teaspoon black pepper

¼ cup warm water (110°F)

2 hard-boiled eggs, chopped

2 tablespoons olive oil

2 oz. fresh parsley, chopped

SOMETHING SWEET

Keto devotees aren't superhumans who have rid themselves of every weakness. Most have the same, oversized sweet tooth that people on normal diets carry. That urge has pushed them to develop some delicious desserts that are ready with minimal effort, ensuring that you can immediately soothe that craving. Sometimes you need to treat yourself—if you've had one of those days, turn to this chapter, and enjoy.

ALMOND FLOUR MUG CAKE

SERVINGS: 1
PREP TIME: 2 MINUTES
COOKING TIME: 5 MINUTES

NUTRITIONAL INFO:
(PER SERVING OF CAKE)
CALORIES: 395
NET CARBS: 4 G
CARBS: 11 G
FAT: 36 G
PROTEIN: 12 G
FIBER: 7 G

NUTRITIONAL INFO:
(PER SERVING OF GANACHE)
CALORIES: 125
NET CARBS: 2 G
CARBS: 3 G
FAT: 18 G
PROTEIN: 1 G
FIBER: 1 G

This recipe is for the folks who just want a quick and easy dessert that doesn't require much baking experience, but still gives a fantastic result.

1. To prepare the cake, place the butter, cream, egg, and vanilla in a mug and stir to combine. Add the almond flour, cocoa powder, salt, and sweetener and stir until thoroughly combined. Place the mug in the microwave and microwave on high for 1 minute. Remove, turn the mug over, and tap it until the cake slides out.

2. To prepare the ganache, place the chocolate and butter in a small bowl and microwave on high for 20 seconds. Remove, stir in the cream and sweetener, and drizzle over the cake. Top with strawberries, if desired, and serve.

FOR THE MUG CAKE

1 teaspoon unsalted butter, melted

1 teaspoon heavy cream

1 egg

¼ teaspoon pure vanilla extract

0.8 oz. almond flour

2 teaspoons unsweetened cocoa powder

Pinch of kosher salt

Stevia or preferred keto-friendly sweetener, to taste

Sliced strawberries, for topping (optional)

FOR THE GANACHE

½ oz. 85 percent or higher dark chocolate, chopped

2 teaspoons unsalted butter

1 teaspoon heavy cream

Stevia or preferred keto-friendly sweetener, to taste

COCONUT FLOUR MUG CAKE

SERVINGS: 1
PREP TIME: 5 MINUTES
COOKING TIME: 5 MINUTES

**NUTRITIONAL INFO:
(PER SERVING
OF CAKE)**

CALORIES: 218

NET CARBS: 3 G

CARBS: 8 G

FAT: 17 G

PROTEIN: 5 G

FIBER: 5 G

**NUTRITIONAL INFO:
(PER SERVING
OF GANACHE)**

CALORIES: 156

NET CARBS: 1 G

CARBS: 3 G

FAT: 21 G

PROTEIN: 3 G

FIBER: 2 G

Coconut flour
provides the perfect
canvas for a vanilla
cake, and you
can add whatever
toppings you want.

1. To prepare the cake, combine all of the ingredients in a mug, place it in the microwave, and microwave on high for 1½ minutes. Remove, turn the mug over, and tap it until the cake falls out.

2. To prepare the ganache, place the butter and peanut butter in a bowl and microwave for 1 minute. Remove and stir to combine. Add the cocoa powder, sweetener, and coconut milk, and stir until thoroughly combined. Drizzle over the cake and serve.

FOR THE CAKE

1 oz. coconut flour

2 tablespoons unsalted butter

2 teaspoons coconut milk

½ teaspoon pure vanilla extract

¼ teaspoon baking powder

1 egg

Stevia or preferred keto-friendly sweetener, to taste

Pinch of kosher salt

FOR THE GANACHE

1½ teaspoons unsalted butter or cocoa butter

1½ teaspoons natural, no sugar added peanut butter

½ teaspoon unsweetened cocoa powder

Stevia, to taste

½ teaspoon coconut milk

BERRY MUG CAKE

SERVINGS: 1
PREP TIME: 5 MINUTES
COOKING TIME: 15 MINUTES

NUTRITIONAL INFO:
(PER SERVING)
CALORIES: 627
NET CARBS: 10 G
CARBS: 15 G
FAT: 55 G
PROTEIN: 12 G
FIBER: 5 G

Use this recipe to turn a plain vanilla mug cake into a very berry treat that pairs perfectly with the vanilla-and-mascarpone frosting.

1. To prepare the berry compote, place all of the ingredients in a saucepan and cook over low heat, stirring occasionally, until the mixture is the consistency of jam. Remove the pan from heat and let the compote cool.

2. To prepare the frosting, place all of the ingredients in a mixing bowl and until beat until a thick frosting forms. Pour the mixture into a piping bag and chill until ready to use.

3. To prepare the mug cake, place all of the ingredients in a mug or ramekin and whisk until combined. Microwave on high for 2½ to 3 minutes, until a toothpick inserted into the center comes out clean. Top with the frosting and compote and serve immediately.

FOR THE BERRY COMPOTE

3.5 oz. blackberries, pureed and strained

3.5 oz. raspberries, pureed and strained

2 teaspoons powdered erythritol

FOR THE FROSTING

0.8 oz. mascarpone cheese, at room temperature

0.8 oz. heavy cream

¼ teaspoon pure vanilla extract

Stevia or preferred keto-friendly sweetener, to taste

FOR THE MUG CAKE

1 teaspoon coconut flour

½ teaspoon baking powder

2 teaspoons berry compote

1 teaspoon heavy cream

2 teaspoons unsalted butter

Stevia or preferred keto-friendly sweetener, to taste

1 egg

PEANUT BUTTER MUG CAKE

SERVINGS: 1
PREP TIME: 2 MINUTES
COOKING TIME: 2 MINUTES

**NUTRITIONAL INFO:
(PER SERVING
WITHOUT WHIPPED
CREAM)**
CALORIES: 533
NET CARBS: 9 G
CARBS: 16 G
FAT: 47 G
PROTEIN: 21 G
FIBER: 7 G

Think of this as a keto-friendly peanut butter cup.

1. Place all of the ingredients, other than the whipped cream, in a mug and whisk until smooth.

2. Microwave for 1 minute and top with whipped cream, if desired.

2.1 oz. natural, no sugar added peanut butter

2 teaspoons unsweetened cocoa powder

1 teaspoon unsalted butter, melted

1 egg

1 teaspoon heavy cream

½ teaspoon baking powder

Stevia or preferred keto-friendly sweetener, to taste

Whipped cream, for garnish (optional)

COFFEE CAKES

SERVINGS: 2
PREP TIME: 5 MINUTES
COOKING TIME: 5 MINUTES

**NUTRITIONAL INFO:
(PER SERVING)**
CALORIES: 294
NET CARBS: 3 G
CARBS: 5 G
FAT: 28 G
PROTEIN: 7 G
FIBER: 2 G

Coffee is a flavor for all seasons, and these cakes capture that beautifully.

1. To begin preparations for the cakes, place the butter in a bowl and microwave for 20 seconds, until it has melted. Stir in the cream, erythritol, and instant coffee powder. If the instant coffee does not dissolve, microwave for another 15 seconds and stir until it does.

2. Add the vanilla, salt, and egg and stir until thoroughly combined. Add the baking powder, almond flour, psyllium husk, and cocoa powder and stir until the mixture is a smooth batter. Divide the batter between two ramekins or mugs and microwave for a minute each. Remove and let cool.

3. To prepare the frosting, place all of the ingredients in a small bowl and stir until combined. Spread over the cakes and serve.

FOR THE CAKES

1 tablespoon unsalted butter

1 oz. heavy cream

1 teaspoon powdered erythritol

1 teaspoon instant coffee powder

½ teaspoon pure vanilla extract

Pinch of kosher salt

1 egg

½ teaspoon baking powder

0.7 oz. almond flour

2 teaspoons psyllium husk

1 teaspoon unsweetened cocoa powder

FOR THE FROSTING

0.8 oz. mascarpone cheese

0.8 oz. heavy cream

¼ teaspoon pure vanilla extract

Stevia, to taste

LEMON & RICOTTA TEA CAKE

SERVINGS: 8
PREP TIME: 10 MINUTES
COOKING TIME: 50 MINUTES

NUTRITIONAL INFO:
(PER SERVING)
CALORIES: 194
NET CARBS: 2 G
CARBS: 3 G
FAT: 18 G
PROTEIN: 6 G
FIBER: 1 G

A rustic but delicate keto cake, which brings a slice of Italy in the summer to your plate.

1. Preheat the oven to 320°F and grease a square 8-inch cake pan with nonstick cooking spray. Place the butter, sweetener, and vanilla in a bowl and beat with a handheld mixer until pale and fluffy. If using a granulated sweetener, make sure to grind it into a fine powder in the blender before using, so that it has an easier time dissolving. Incorporate the eggs one at a time and beat until frothy. Stir in the ricotta and lemon zest and juice and set the mixture aside.

2. Sift the almond flour and baking powder into a separate bowl and stir, making sure there are no lumps. Working in two batches, stir the dry mixture into the wet mixture.

3. Pour the batter into the pan and place it in the oven. Bake for about 50 minutes, until a toothpick inserted into the center comes up with only a few crumbs. Remove and let the cake cool before slicing. Garnish with slivered almonds and lemon slices before serving.

2.8 oz. unsalted butter

3.5 oz. Sukrin Gold or preferred keto-friendly sweetener

1 teaspoon pure vanilla extract

3 eggs

5.3 oz. ricotta cheese

Zest and juice of 1 lemon

3.5 oz. almond flour

1 teaspoon baking powder

Slivered almonds, for garnish

Lemon slices, for garnish

ETON MESS

SERVINGS: 4
PREP TIME: 5 MINUTES
COOKING TIME: 35 MINUTES

NUTRITIONAL INFO:
(PER SERVING)
CALORIES: 146
NET CARBS: 2 G
CARBS: 3 G
FAT: 14 G
PROTEIN: 3 G
FIBER: 1 G

Layers of chewy meringue complement the incredible combination of strawberries and cream in this elegant dessert.

1. Preheat the oven to 245°F and line a baking sheet with parchment paper. Place the egg whites in a bowl and beat until frothy. Add the cream of tartar and beat until soft peaks form. Add half of the vanilla and the erythritol and whisk to combine.

2. Transfer the mixture to the baking sheet and bake for 30 to 35 minutes, until cooked through. Remove and let the meringue cool for 15 minutes before removing it from the parchment paper.

3. While the meringue is in the oven, place the heavy cream, stevia, and the remaining vanilla in a bowl and beat until soft peaks form. Refrigerate for 15 minutes and then fold the strawberries into the mixture. Break the meringue into pieces, add it to the strawberries and cream, and serve.

2 egg whites

¼ teaspoon cream of tartar

1 teaspoon pure vanilla extract

1½ teaspoons powdered erythritol

5.3 oz. heavy cream

Stevia or preferred keto-friendly sweetener, to taste

3.5 oz. strawberries, hulled and diced

COFFEE & CHOCOLATE TARTS

SERVINGS: 3
PREP TIME: 5 MINUTES
COOKING TIME: 10 MINUTES

NUTRITIONAL INFO:
(PER SERVING)
CALORIES: 490
NET CARBS: 3 G
CARBS: 7 G
FAT: 49 G
PROTEIN: 8 G
FIBER: 4 G

These tarts layer chocolate ganache and a coffee-mascarpone crème on a crisp chocolate-almond flour base for a dessert that will always have you going back for seconds (or thirds).

1. Preheat the oven to 350°F. Place the almond flour, cocoa powder, sweetener, vanilla, and butter in a mixing bowl and stir until the mixture has the consistency of wet sand.

2. Divide the mixture between three ramekins and press it into their bases. Bake for 10 minutes, remove from the oven, and let them cool slightly. Dissolve the instant espresso powder in the hot water and let it cool.

3. Place the mascarpone cheese, more sweetener, and the coffee in a bowl and beat until nice and fluffy. Pour the mascarpone mixture over the cooled tart bases and refrigerate for 10 minutes.

4. Microwave the heavy cream for 30 seconds. Add the chocolate and more sweetener and stir until you have a creamy ganache. Pour the ganache over the coffee-mascarpone crème and refrigerate for an hour.

5. Sprinkle sea salt over the tarts and serve.

1.5 oz. almond flour

1 teaspoon unsweetened cocoa powder

Stevia or preferred keto-friendly sweetener, to taste

1 teaspoon pure vanilla extract

2 tablespoons salted butter, melted

1 teaspoon instant espresso powder

2 tablespoons hot water (125°F)

5.3 oz. mascarpone cheese

3.5 oz. heavy cream

1 oz. 85 percent dark chocolate

Sea salt, to taste

CHOCOLATE MOUSSE

SERVINGS: 4
PREP TIME: 5 MINUTES
REFRIGERATION TIME: 1 HOUR

NUTRITIONAL INFO: (PER SERVING)
CALORIES: 239
NET CARBS: 2 G
CARBS: 6 G
FAT: 22 G
PROTEIN: 3 G
FIBER: 4 G

Few things are as decadent as chocolate mousse. And nothing has an easier time getting to that rarefied air.

1. Place the chocolate and butter in a microwave-safe bowl and microwave for 30 seconds. Remove, stir to combine, and let cool.

2. Place the cream, cocoa powder, sweetener, and chocolate mixture in a mixing bowl and beat until soft peaks form.

3. Divide the mousse between serving bowls and refrigerate for at least an hour before serving.

1.75 oz. 85 percent dark chocolate

1 tablespoon unsalted butter

7 oz. heavy cream

1 teaspoon unsweetened cocoa powder

Stevia or preferred keto-friendly sweetener, to taste

PANNA COTTA

SERVINGS: 3
PREP TIME: 5 MINUTES
REFRIGERATION TIME:
4 HOURS

NUTRITIONAL INFO:
(PER SERVING)
CALORIES: 204
NET CARBS: 3 G
CARBS: 3 G
FAT: 20 G
PROTEIN: 3 G
FIBER: 0 G

A well-made panna cotta has the slightest wobble—it should gently shimmy when you shake it—and a texture that absolutely melts in your mouth.

1. Place the gelatin and the water in a mug and let the mixture sit for 5 minutes.

2. Pour the cream into a small saucepan and warm over low heat. Add the sweetener and stir until dissolved. Add the vanilla seeds and pod and stir to combine. When the cream comes to a simmer, remove the pan from heat and discard the vanilla pod. Add the gelatin mixture to the cream and stir until completely dissolved.

3. Pour the mixture into ramekins and chill in the refrigerator for at least 4 hours. To unmold the panna cotta after they are set, dip the molds halfway into a bowl of hot water, then upend onto a plate. Top with mixed berries before serving.

1 teaspoon gelatin

2 tablespoons water

3.9 oz. heavy cream

Stevia or preferred keto-friendly sweetener, to taste

Seeds and pod from 1 vanilla bean

Mixed berries, for topping

POT DE CRÈME

SERVINGS: 2
PREP TIME: 5 MINUTES
COOKING TIME: 10 MINUTES

NUTRITIONAL INFO:
(PER SERVING
WITHOUT TOPPING)
CALORIES: 345
NET CARBS: 6 G
CARBS: 10 G
FAT: 34 G
PROTEIN: 5 G
FIBER: 4 G

You can serve this warm or, if you're more patient than most, wait for it to set in the refrigerator, where it becomes a chocolate truffle.

1. Break the chocolate into small pieces and place them in a bowl. Place the egg yolk in a separate bowl and give it a quick whisk.

2. Place the cream, erythritol, and vanilla in a saucepan and warm over low heat while stirring constantly. As soon as bubbles appear in the cream, remove the pan from heat. Add a spoonful of the hot cream to the egg yolk and whisk to combine. Stir the tempered yolk into the saucepan and cook the mixture over low heat until it is thick enough to coat the back of a wooden spoon.

3. Pour the custard over the chocolate, add the salt, and let the mixture sit for a minute. Whisk until the mixture is a thick pudding and, if desired, top with whipped cream, crème fraiche, or berry compote.

12.1 oz. Baker's Chocolate

1 egg yolk

2.8 oz. heavy cream, plus more as needed

1½ teaspoons powdered erythritol

2 to 3 drops of pure vanilla extract

Pinch of kosher salt

Whipped cream or crème fraîche, for topping (optional)

Berry compote, for topping (optional, see page 227)

TIRAMISU

SERVINGS: 8
PREP TIME: 10 MINUTES
REFRIGERATION TIME:
10 MINUTES

**NUTRITIONAL INFO:
(PER SERVING)**
CALORIES: 308
NET CARBS: 5 G
CARBS: 6 G
FAT: 29 G
PROTEIN: 16 G
FIBER: 1 G

Being able to eat tiramisu and lose weight—this must be heaven.

1. Place the espresso, whiskey, and cream in a bowl and stir to combine. Place the egg white in a bowl and beat until stiff peaks form. Set aside.

2. Place the egg yolk and sweetener in a separate bowl and whisk until the mixture is a pale yellow. Add the mascarpone cheese and 2.1 oz. of the espresso mixture and whisk until it becomes a smooth custard. Working in two batches, fold in the beaten egg white.

3. Slice the bread as desired and then dip the slices into the remaining espresso mixture. Layer them in a baking dish, pour the custard over the top, and refrigerate until set, about 10 minutes. Dust with the cocoa powder before serving.

2.1 oz. brewed espresso

1 oz. whiskey (optional)

1 oz. heavy cream

1 egg, yolk and white separated

Stevia or preferred keto-friendly sweetener, to taste

14 oz. mascarpone cheese

2 portions of Mug Bread (see page 45)

2 teaspoons unsweetened cocoa powder

CHOCOLATE CHIA PUDDING

SERVINGS: 4
PREP TIME: 5 MINUTES
REFRIGERATION TIME:
12 HOURS

NUTRITIONAL INFO:
(PER SERVING)
CALORIES: 296
NET CARBS: 7.2 G
CARBS: 28.7 G
FAT: 18.5 G
PROTEIN: 12.9 G
FIBER: 21.5 G

Place this in the refrigerator the night before and you'll come home with a nutritious treat ready to-go.

1. Place the chia seeds, almond milk, and sweetener in a mixing bowl and stir to combine. Cover the bowl and let the mixture stand at room temperature for 30 minutes.

2. Stir the mixture and then sift the cacao powder over it, while stirring constantly. Divide the mixture between four serving glasses, cover, and refrigerate overnight.

3. Top each portion with some of the yogurt, berries, and chocolate.

5.6 oz. chia seeds

2½ cups unsweetened almond milk

2 tablespoons stevia or preferred keto-friendly sweetener

1.2 oz. unsweetened cocoa powder

¼ cup Greek yogurt

0.8 oz. blueberries

1 oz. blackberries

1 tablespoon sugar-free bittersweet chocolate

ORANGE CHIA PUDDING WITH PISTACHIOS

SERVINGS: 4
PREP TIME: 5 MINUTES
REFRIGERATION TIME:
12 HOURS

NUTRITIONAL INFO:
(PER SERVING)
CALORIES: 358
NET CARBS: 4.9 G
CARBS: 17.5 G
FAT: 29.7 G
PROTEIN: 12.1 G
FIBER: 12.6 G

This pudding will also work for breakfast if you're looking for a sweet start to the day.

1. Place the coconut milk, almond milk, chia seeds, sweetener, and orange blossom water in a mixing bowl and stir to combine. Cover and refrigerate overnight.

2. Stir the orange juice into the pudding. Divide between the serving bowls and sprinkle the pistachios on top of each portion.

2 cups coconut milk

2 cups unsweetened almond milk

1.4 oz. white chia seeds

1.4 oz. black chia seeds, plus 1 tablespoon

1 tablespoon stevia or preferred keto-friendly sweetener

½ teaspoon orange blossom water

Juice of ½ orange

1.75 oz. chopped unsalted pistachios

COCONUT BLISS BALLS

SERVINGS: 12
PREP TIME: 5 MINUTES
FREEZING TIME: 20 MINUTES

**NUTRITIONAL INFO:
(PER SERVING)**
CALORIES: 212
NET CARBS: 4.3 G
CARBS: 6.5 G
FAT: 20.7 G
PROTEIN: 3 G
FIBER: 2.2 G

Fans of coconut's creamy sweetness get all they could ever want in this simple preparation.

1. Place the coconut oil, almond butter, and maple syrup in a bowl and stir to combine. Stir in two-thirds of the coconut, the almonds, vanilla, and salt, cover the bowl, and freeze until set, about 20 minutes.

2. Place the remaining coconut in a shallow dish. Form 2-tablespoon portions of the mixture into balls and roll them in the coconut. Serve immediately or store in the refrigerator.

½ cup coconut oil, melted

½ cup almond butter, melted

2 tablespoons real maple syrup

3.2 oz. unsweetened shredded coconut

1.75 oz. almonds, chopped

½ teaspoon pure vanilla extract

Pinch of kosher salt

METRIC CONVERSIONS

U.S. Measurement	Approximate Metric Liquid Measurement	Approximate Metric Dry Measurement
1 teaspoon	5 ml	5 g
1 tablespoon or ½ ounce	15 ml	14 g
1 ounce or ⅛ cup	30 ml	29 g
¼ cup or 2 ounces	60 ml	57 g
⅓ cup	80 ml	76 g
½ cup or 4 ounces	120 ml	113 g
⅔ cup	160 ml	151 g
¾ cup or 6 ounces	180 ml	170 g
1 cup or 8 ounces or ½ pint	240 ml	227 g
1½ cups or 12 ounces	350 ml	340 g
2 cups or 1 pint or 16 ounces	475 ml	454 g
3 cups or 1½ pints	700 ml	680 g
4 cups or 2 pints or 1 quart	950 ml	908 g

INDEX

ABOUT CIDER MILL PRESS BOOK PUBLISHERS

Good ideas ripen with time. From seed to harvest, Cider Mill Press brings fine reading, information, and entertainment together between the covers of its creatively crafted books. Our Cider Mill bears fruit twice a year, publishing a new crop of titles each spring and fall.

"Where Good Books Are Ready for Press"

VISIT US ON THE WEB AT
cidermillpress.com

OR WRITE TO US AT
PO Box 454
12 Spring St.
Kennebunkport, Maine 04046